MORE ADVANCE PRAISE
FOR PEACE @ WORK

"The four-step process in *Peace @ Work* is an incredibly helpful tool for anyone to use. Leaders can effectively apply these principles in their own work and they can coach others to deal directly with relationship issues when they arise. This book provides a practical guide on how to improve communication and teamwork, which is the cornerstone of high quality care."

— KATIE KESSLER, MSN, RN,
Michigan Center for Nursing

PT CONSULTING GROUP, LLC

PT CONSULTING GROUP, LLC IS A WORKPLACE CONSULTING COMPANY FOCUSED ON ASSISTING IN THE AREAS OF EMPLOYEE AND LEADERSHIP DEVELOPMENT THROUGH ASSESSMENTS, TRAINING AND COACHING. AREAS OF FOCUS INCLUDE COMMUNICATION SKILLS, TEAMWORK, DEALING WITH NEGATIVITY IN THE WORKPLACE, AND CONFLICT RESOLUTION.

WWW.PT-CONSULTING-GROUP.COM

PEACE
@
WORK

PEACE

@

WORK

A SHORT, PRACTICAL
AND EASY-TO-REMEMBER GUIDE
FOR RESOLVING CONFLICTS
AT WORK

PAM THEISEN

PT CONSULTING GROUP, LLC
BLOOMFIELD, MICHIGAN

Published by
PT Consulting Group, LLC
Bloomfield, Michigan
www.pt-consulting-group.com

Publisher's Cataloging-in-Publication Data
Theisen, Pam.

  Peace at work : a short, practical and easy-to-remember guide
  for resolving conflicts at work / by Pam Theisen. – Bloomfield,
  MI : PT Consulting Group, LLC, 2013.

  p. ; cm.

  ISBN13: 978-0-9860368-0-4

  1. Conflict management. 2. Interpersonal relations.
  3. Communication in management. 4. Interpersonal
  communication. I. Title.

HD42.T44 2013
650.13—dc23   2013904137

Project coordination by Jenkins Group, Inc.
www.BookPublishing.com

cover design by Chris Rhoads
interior design by Yvonne Fetig Roehler

Printed in the United States of America
17 16 15 14 13 • 5 4 3 2 1

"The single biggest problem with communication
is the illusion that it has taken place."

— George Bernard Shaw

CONTENTS

WHAT DO PEOPLE WANT?

Peace at work.

It's something most people say they want. We spend a lot of time at work, and we interact with a broad spectrum of people as part of our jobs. This includes people who are easy to get along with, people who are incredibly difficult to deal with, and people who are somewhere in between.

We deal with young people at the beginning of their careers who dream of rapid advancement, older people near the end of their careers who are proudly heading for retirement, people who work with some level of passion and commitment and those who don't care much about anything besides collecting a paycheck.

We encounter people who are very successful and freely help others in need and also those who feel stuck in their jobs or who believe they are a victim of their jobs or of someone in their work life. Often, these individuals seem to want to share their unhappiness with anyone who will listen.

We spend so much time at work that many of us see more of our colleagues than our own family members. Consequently, when we encounter conflict at work that is difficult to resolve, it impacts our moods, our attitudes, and also our personal lives.

It's important to maintain a peaceful work environment for many reasons, the biggest of which is our health. Stress causes a lot of hardship, both physically and mentally, and increased mental stress is something most want to avoid. Indeed, just meeting the demands of our jobs can cause significant stress. We do not need the added burden of worrying about those with whom we have to work.

Based on my experiences in the workplace, I believe the key to decreasing stress and increasing general contentment at work lies in communication. The truth is, anyone who has a desire to improve their relationships at work can learn communication skills that allow them to do exactly this.

That said, let me comment that while I often hear people talk about how difficult they find other people to be, the truth is that we can all be difficult at times. The part of the population that is truly awful to deal with is really a small minority. In my experience, most people can be reasonable when there is open and positive communication.

I've had the benefit of an extensive career in a large and complex academic health care organization. I started my career as a social worker fresh out of a master's program working with oncology and then heart transplant patients. Coming from a small town and being young and inexperienced in a vast, ethnically diverse inner city hospital quickly taught me to be an effective communicator. I realized very early that I either had to become more assertive or I needed to find a new field.

Eventually, I moved to developing and then managing an employee assistance program (EAP) that offered a wide range of services for our health care organization and others, including counseling, training, and consulting on problem resolution. From there, a variety of management, employee and leadership development, and customer service positions followed.

Today I work as an independent consultant doing training, coaching, and other related work. Throughout my thirty-year career, I've worked with numerous individuals and departments to help resolve conflicts and work performance problems related to customer service and interpersonal problems within teams. Each of these experiences helped me to hone the four-part technique I use today in my training and coaching program to help people make necessary improvements in how they communicate on the job.

You might be wondering if the world really needs another book on the subject of conflict resolution or, to put it more graphically, if the world really needs another book on how to deal with people you dislike or simply can't stand.

I believe it does, for the simple reason that existing books and typical conflict resolution training sessions look good on paper but are too complicated to be practical.

The fact is, any approach requiring seven, eight, or nine steps is too cumbersome to be of use. After all, you typically need to be able to remember this information when you're in a critical or high-stress situation. How many steps are you going to be able to remember in the midst of a crisis?

To simplify conflict resolution at work is the primary reason I wrote *Peace @ Work*. I like simplicity and practicality. As someone who has spent three decades training, counseling, and coaching others, I know firsthand that keeping it simple is essential. The technique that I present in this book is short and easy to remember. I've used it a great deal over the years and have had excellent results from people who've told me it has helped them to stay focused on what's important. I've also been told many times that it not only works on the job but at home as well.

After so many years in this field, I can truly say I've seen almost everything. I've witnessed people at all levels in complex organizations with incredible talents and abilities lose their jobs or reputations because of their lack of interpersonal skills. These individuals didn't always know how to interact on a professional level when confronted by people they found difficult, and that's the second reason I wrote this book. I truly enjoy people, and most of the individuals I've encountered in the workplace are nice, talented, and hard working. It's a shame for them to ever feel victimized at work or to find themselves out of a job because they never learned how to communicate effectively when they encounter a problem.

Peace @ Work addresses this need. It is concise, practical, and short. It is easy to digest and integrate, and it can permanently and positively alter your approach to handling conflict in the workplace.

The book combines stories with content to help reinforce key points. It begins with a story from early in my career that demonstrates how easy it is to add to workplace conflicts without much awareness that you're doing so. The next several chapters present four colleagues whose personalities and communication styles foreshadow the inevitable challenges they face when they begin working with another department within the same company and their supervisor is replaced. Their experiences help highlight the importance of focusing on yourself and your own communication when confronted with difficult colleagues and supervisors. The book concludes with several appendices that contain the conflict resolution technique in outline form, additional short story examples that help to reinforce the key points, a troubleshooting section that answers common questions, and a short review to help you retain key information.

As you read the stories contained in *Peace @ Work*, you may wonder if they are based on real people and situations. The answer is yes. Many times in my career, people have jokingly asked if I have been spying on their department. I reply that the types of workplace conflicts and department dramas I've seen over the years play out repeatedly in all types of work environments. The people, situations, and circumstances change, but the underlying issue tends to remain the same – a lack of straightforward communication that successfully addresses the root problem. The longer this continues, the more complicated the problem becomes, until it is blown completely out of proportion and dysfunctional relationships prevail. This is often the point at which consultants like me are called in.

Like most people, I've experienced my share of work-related conflicts. Early in my career, I made a few classic communication mistakes that I've since learned from. Because life would have been much easier had I known to follow the key points presented in this book, it is my fervent hope that my experience can help others learn the communication skills that will keep them from compounding whatever work-related problems they face.

The good news is, most people do not stay awake at night scheming about how to make their colleagues miserable the next day. They don't go to bed thinking, "I can't wait to get up, go to work, and purposely irritate everyone I come into contact with." On the contrary, most people want to go to work and do a good job while having positive interactions with their colleagues and customers.

In other words, they want peace at work.

CHAPTER ONE

A LACK OF COMMUNICATION, TIM'S STORY

Most of us will find ourselves at odds with a colleague or supervisor at some point in our work history. How we deal with it can have significant consequences. We can choose to do what we can to improve the situation, or we can choose another path. If we fail to focus on what's important and instead avoid the situation, the problem can escalate or even perpetuate, as the following story relays.

Tim had only been in his current job for two years when he came to see me about a problem he was having at work. This was his first professional job after college and things weren't going well for him. He worked in an IT department and he recalled how excited he was to get a great job right out of school. He couldn't understand how things had deteriorated to this point. He explained that he just wanted to be able to go to work, do his job, and work in peace.

There were many things Tim liked about his work, and he'd hoped to continue growing his career within this organization. He loved the company, what it stood for, the culture, and most of the people.

The only person Tim didn't get along with was his boss. In fact, he hated this person for bringing disciplinary actions against him based on a work performance issue.

This was a huge blow for Tim. He felt embarrassed, at risk, and confused. He was also incredibly angry. He admitted that he hadn't been sleeping well and that his wife was concerned about him.

As he explained what he'd been dealing with, Tim's face became red with anger. He explained that he held his boss accountable for what was happening but that he refused to let this "loser" cost him his job and his future.

When I asked Tim what he planned to do about the problem, he continued to stare straight ahead for several seconds, a glare distorting his features. Finally he replied that he wasn't sure; all he knew was that things needed to get better quickly.

Tim had come to talk to me about the same thing so many others had: conflict on the job. He needed help, and that was what I was there for. That's when we started to talk about his options.

I asked Tim what options he thought he had. His first response was to hope his boss would disappear in some magical way. He then told me he'd thought of quitting, but he and his wife had agreed this wasn't a good time to walk away from a job. Besides, they were aware that it's much easier to find another job when you already have one.

He'd thought of writing a letter to the head of the department and also to the head of human resources, but he realized this would likely only make his situation worse.

Tim then added that he could just continue to cope with the situation as it was and hope that things improved with time.

When I asked how likely that outcome was, he stated that he wasn't sure but the odds obviously weren't in his favor.

I told Tim he was missing an option and he looked at me blankly. I told him he could talk honestly with his boss and try to figure out how they could improve their relationship.

At this point, Tim's face began to scare me. Now he began glaring at me.

"I can't improve my relationship with him. He hates me and I hate him!" he practically yelled.

"Okay," I stated. "Let's talk about why that's the case."

"Oh, I can tell you why," Tim responded caustically. "It's because he's an insecure, bitter man with no sensitivity to other people. No one can stand that jerk."

I asked Tim to explain how and why he'd been written up, and he told a doleful tale of how he'd been victimized by his boss. The story was pretty convincing. Tim's boss did indeed appear to be completely at fault and an absolute jerk, just as Tim said.

Then again, it's usually that way. The person telling the story makes the other person out to be a villain, while the storyteller is an innocent victim. I've told that tale myself in the past.

After explaining that he'd been written up for a work report that was late due to a communication problem, Tim added that he couldn't do anything right. His boss simply disliked him and had it in for him.

I asked Tim why he thought his boss disliked him and at first he stated that he wasn't sure. Then he added that perhaps his boss was jealous. Tim explained that his boss wasn't very knowledgeable about many critical areas in IT, that he was primarily a finance person who had been transplanted to the IT department. While he knew enough to get by, Tim explained, he certainly wasn't as knowledgeable as Tim.

Tim relayed his boss's shortcomings with great enthusiasm, happier than he'd appeared at any other point in our meeting.

He added that he could tell his boss didn't like him by the way he talked to him. He was much more upbeat with others on the team and went out of his way to greet them while he all but ignored Tim. During meetings, his boss seemed to skip over anything Tim said without comment but he frequently complimented colleagues who offered less. As Tim described the repeated slights he felt he experienced from his boss, he stated that he felt increasingly tense and uncomfortable at work.

"I think he just wants me out of the department. It's that simple," he finally concluded.

Tim now looked quite sad as he communicated how unfair this was to him. He just didn't understand why this was happening. After all, he reiterated, he just wanted to come to work and work in peace, not constant tension and stress.

I asked Tim to go back to why he felt his boss disliked him and again he repeated that his boss wasn't very knowledgeable about IT. Tim further explained that he could run circles around his boss and his boss knew it.

I asked Tim if this knowledge impacted his behavior towards his boss in any way.

Tim became very quiet for several seconds and then replied, "Well, I can't stand the guy so I make sure I let him know when he's wrong. When we have meetings, I make sure to speak up if he doesn't know or understand something. He's so clueless, I often look at my colleagues and we smile and roll our eyes at how stupid he can be sometimes. We all feel the same way about him."

At this point, I again asked Tim what he wanted from his job. He repeated that he just wanted to work in peace.

"Are you sure that's all you want?" I asked.

Tim nodded and said, "Of course. I've been saying that since I sat down with you."

"Well, if you're so sure, then let me ask you a few questions to help clarify everything I've heard, okay?"

"Sure," Tim said.

"You say that you just want to be able to do your job and work in peace."

"Yes, repeatedly."

"The problem keeping you from this is your boss."

"Yes."

"You believe he treats you unfairly in the department because he doesn't like you."

"Exactly."

"The reason you feel this way is that your boss doesn't talk to you much, rarely acknowledges you, yet seems very friendly with your colleagues, and now he's written you up for a work performance issue that you say is invalid."

"Don't forget that he's a jerk."

"Yes, and you feel that he does this because he's an insecure, insensitive jerk who isn't very knowledgeable in his position."

"Correct."

"You on the other hand are very smart and know a lot about the work of the department. You are a true IT person while your boss is not."

"You got it."

"And the way you've handled this is by flaunting your knowledge in your boss's face and occasionally rolling your eyes and bonding with your colleagues over his shortcomings during meetings."

"I didn't say that."

"I think you did."

"I didn't use the word 'flaunt' or talk about bonding."

Tim's story is pretty common. People get into all types of conflicts at work, and too often they focus on the other person or people as the source of the problem.

From my perspective, it's better to look at yourself to determine exactly what you are doing and what you need to do differently. Often, that will involve having a conversation with the person you're in conflict with to help solve whatever problem might exist.

Tim didn't do this. Instead, he allowed built-up resentment and frustration to contribute to an already difficult relationship. As time went by and the problem progressed, he failed to take any action to help resolve it. He was too focused on being angry and placing all the blame on his boss.

My judgment was that Tim's behavior was inconsistent with what he said he wanted. If he truly wanted to go to work and do his job in peace, he needed to make sure that he was doing what was necessary to achieve peace.

Tim and I discussed his situation a little further and determined that solving the problem would require him to initiate a conversation with his boss. He accepted this, but he felt incapable of following through for several reasons, many of them fear-based. He didn't want to cause more difficulty in the already difficult relationship, so he continued allowing the negative relationship to build and vented elsewhere to cope. The fact that he was already working every day in some fear seemed less important to him than contemplating this discussion with his boss.

I recommended that Tim think about the situation and come back to me if he decided to address it. I reassured him that with a couple of key steps guiding him, he could have a conversation with his boss that would prove to be very helpful in getting to a resolution.

Tim assured me that he would think about it and would call if and when he decided he was ready to pursue that conversation.

He phoned me about two months later to tell me he'd taken another job and was much happier to be away from the jerk boss he'd suffered through. All was going well, he reported, with the exception of one colleague who seemed manipulative and possibly untrustworthy. Tim stated that he'd need more time to figure this colleague out, but he was sure he'd be easier to deal with than his former boss.

He thanked me for my time and I wished him great success, but my experience with Tim told me his career was going to be more of a challenge than he anticipated. Focusing his attention on other peoples' shortcomings and avoiding straightforward conversations were two surefire ways to make work harder for himself.

I hung up the phone wishing Tim had taken the opportunity to learn to problem-solve more directly when he had a problem on the job. He had an opportunity to learn and grow from the conflict with his boss. He had a chance to gain insight into how to problem-solve with people he finds difficult.

His reluctance to do so is classic. He chose to take what seemed like an easier path, but I suspect that his lack of self-awareness and insight could result in additional challenges down the road if he continues to focus on other people's behavior instead of on what he can do differently to resolve problems.

While it can be quite disturbing to work for someone you feel uncomfortable with and possibly even threatened by, failing to even attempt to resolve ongoing issues creates a lot of additional and unnecessary stress both at work and at home. Because we don't have control over other people, it is beneficial to look at our own behavior and what we can do differently. Often this will involve initiating a conversation. From my perspective, understanding the many reasons people avoid such conversations is an important step toward helping them rethink this approach.

WHY IS RESOLVING CONFLICTS AT WORK SO DIFFICULT?

Famed psychologist Albert Ellis told us in the 1950s that people don't always think rationally. I frequently see this in the workplace, where irrational thinking can cause numerous problems. We human beings develop our beliefs over many years, and some of these beliefs become hardwired in our thinking. In turn, what we tell ourselves is incredibly powerful in determining our behavior. The problem is, what we tell ourselves isn't always true. Indeed, as the following examples illustrate, our irrational thinking can prevent us from effectively problem-solving when faced with a conflict or a person we find difficult.

We believe other people know exactly how irritating, how obnoxious, how upsetting, or how wrong they are. In this regard, kids have an advantage over adults. Children are typically more forgiving than adults and are also more willing to tell others exactly what they think. This can be tough to take, but at least when we're dealing with children we know where we stand!

As we age, we typically become more discreet and diplomatic. As a result, we often keep our judgments and more importantly our feedback to ourselves, or we decide to share our discontent with only a few select others. See if the following conversation between Bill and his wife Sue is similar to what you sometimes hear or even say yourself about someone else's irritating behavior:

BILL: I work with this guy who is so annoying. All he talks about is sports. If he gives an example, it's related to sports. We could be talking about the weather and he brings up sports. None of us can stand having a conversation with him.

As soon as he starts talking, everyone quickly escapes with excuses. I actually saw him coming down the hallway today and I turned around and walked the other way.

Sue: Have you thought of helping him out and talking to him about the problem?

Bill: Of course not. What would be the point? The guy apparently doesn't know how to talk about anything else, so what good would it do? Someone told me awhile back that she tried to talk to him about it and he just became defensive. I tell you, people like that don't care who they annoy. They are so clueless that there's no getting through to them.

> *If you were doing something that was troubling or bothersome to someone else, would you want to know? Most people answer with, "Of course," yet we often don't use that same thinking or consideration when it comes to people at work or in other situations where there might be a problem.*

How common is this type of situation? In my experience, very common. Conversations like this occur each and every day, with all kinds of variations. The problem is, they reflect questionable assumptions about other people's behavior and motivations while providing various reasons for not talking to them to resolve the problem. One common reason is, "I don't want to hurt the other person's feelings." That thinking is rather odd, because instead of trying to help the person by talking to them, we believe we can avoid hurting their feelings by shunning them in the future or by complaining about them to others.

What are some other reasons people avoid talking to each other about problems they're having in the workplace?

We assume the person already knows how we feel and just doesn't care. This is another great irrational belief that many, like our friend Bill in the previous example, fall victim to.

I remember having a conversation with a colleague many years ago. We were very dependent on each other at work, covering a 24/7 operation, and I was the manager of the department. Since we really needed to support each other, I asked my colleague what I could do to be easier to work with. She didn't have any feedback for me, so I lightly pressed her and asked for her input on one thing I could change that would make working with me easier. After cheerfully asking her to please give me just one thing and then promising to leave her alone, she said, "Well, when I give you something, you could stop snatching it out of my hands."

I looked at her in disbelief and asked if I really did that and, if so, how often. She proceeded to demonstrate my behavior by asking me to give her some paperwork. She quickly and quite rudely snatched it from me and said, "You do it all the time."

I couldn't believe I'd been so clueless, but I'd sincerely had no idea. Needless to say, once I was aware of this habit, I was able to stop snatching papers out of my colleague's hands.

I'd like to tell you this was the only irritating behavior I've been clueless about, but that would be a lie. Over the years, I've gained insight into a few other problems, and I'm grateful for it, because only with awareness have I been able to resolve these issues.

We fear making things worse. Often, people are afraid of the response they might get if they initiate a conversation to resolve a problem. They are afraid a conflict will escalate when avoiding conflict is all they want in the first place. This is a very irrational thought that keeps people from communicating when it's important.

I remember talking to a woman after a presentation who described a problem with her sister who lived in another state. Her sister called every Sunday to "catch up." She told me she'd grown to hate talking to her sister because all she wanted to talk about was herself. She further explained that she would listen patiently, comment, and offer feedback to her sister, but as soon as she tried to talk about her own life, her sister lost interest. She explained that she was almost at the point of not answering the phone any longer because she'd completely lost any desire to talk to her sister.

When she asked for my advice, my first question was whether or not she had talked to her sister about this situation.

The woman looked at me with surprise and said she couldn't do that. When I asked why, she told me she didn't want to upset her sister and make things worse.

Make things worse? She'd just told me she no longer wanted to talk to her sister! In light of that, the fear of making things worse wasn't rational. When I pointed this out, she agreed. Nonetheless, she still didn't feel capable of talking to her sister about the situation.

How sad, I reflected, that she would choose to allow her silence to hurt and possibly destroy this sibling relationship. Unfortunately, this situation is quite common.

We assume it's not going to do any good to let the person know. "He won't change his behavior." "She won't care what I think." "It's just not worth it."

People fall victim to excuses such as these quite easily. One reason is that we often think we've already communicated our concerns. Since the behavior didn't change, why bother to try again?

There are two things to consider here. First is whether you've communicated effectively. I remember a conversation with a colleague who complained that our boss always went way over topic, didn't stick to the agenda, and didn't pay attention to the time. When I asked if she thought our boss was aware of the problem, she said she was certain he knew and just didn't care.

I then asked if she'd talked to him about it. She replied that during meetings, she frequently made eye contact with him and pointed to her watch. She then said, "He just doesn't get it."

Alas, it's not uncommon for people to drop hints and then become frustrated by a lack of response. This colleague felt like she'd done the equivalent of talking to our boss about a problematic behavior, but dropping hints is usually ineffective and can even make *you* appear to be the annoying one.

It's important to remember two main points moving forward. The first is that most people are oblivious to what your concerns are, no matter how it looks or what you may think. Second, even if they have some awareness of a problem, they certainly don't see it from your perspective.

Unfortunately, when someone says or does something we don't like, we often offer our own explanation, and it's usually quite negative. Remember what Bill said about his poor sports-obsessed colleague? Here is the statement: *"Someone told me awhile back that she tried to talk to him about it and he just became defensive. I tell you, people like that don't care who they annoy. They are so clueless that there's no getting through to them."*

The initial problem is that Bill relies on hearsay, or what someone allegedly told someone else. To top it off, Bill assumes his colleague just doesn't care that people find him annoying!

When people make assumptions, jump to conclusions, and avoid having a kind and straightforward discussion, it just adds to the problem.

The workplace is especially ripe for this type of thinking because the environment can be competitive, the pace and stress can be taxing, and we frequently work and interact with many different kinds of people.

> *Most people are oblivious to what your concerns are, no matter how it looks or what you may think, and even if they have some awareness of a problem, they certainly don't see it from your perspective.*

Clear communication can also be a challenge and the opportunity for misunderstandings is quite high, as evidenced by the following types of assumptions or beliefs:

"She didn't acknowledge me because she doesn't like me."

"He ignored me because he's mad at me."

"She didn't offer to help me because she's self-absorbed and never thinks of anyone else."

"He made that comment during the meeting because he doesn't think I know what I'm doing."

The second important point to consider moving forward is that maintaining a positive relationship with someone you deal with in the workplace is in your long-term best interests. Many people build their careers on relationships and reputation. The more capable you are of establishing and maintaining positive relationships with all kinds of people, in spite of your differences, the easier it is to have a successful career. The person you totally tick off early in your career could be someone you find yourself working for later in life. This may sound like a stretch, but it happens. Simply put, burning bridges at work is not the wisest move for career development.

> *In the long run, maintaining a positive relationship with someone you deal with in the workplace is in your best interests.*

In addition, most companies have expectations for their employees regarding teamwork and communication. If you work in a department and do not speak to your colleagues out of spite or pettiness, you put your job at risk. Most companies do not allow this type of behavior to continue unaddressed. Some people do tend to be more shy and introverted, but that's not what I am referring to here. It's when you cannot develop and maintain positive working relationships with others that your career can be hindered or even damaged. This can be especially true if you are planning to develop your career within a large company. Strained relationships will hurt your reputation. It's also important to note that they also make work even more stressful.

Look around at the people you work with and ask yourself what the high achievers have in common. More often than not, you'll see that they have positive relationships with others. Even if you have a job that allows you to work fairly independently, you can't totally escape the reality that your ability to communicate effectively is important.

WHY SHOULD WE CARE ABOUT GETTING ALONG WITH COLLEAGUES?

For numerous reasons, every worker in America and abroad should care about getting along with their colleagues. A few of these reasons are as follows.

Your job satisfaction and overall stress level may depend on it. Workplace conflicts can be taxing for anyone, and they usually don't resolve on their own. In fact, these conflicts can fester and grow over time, along with your stress level. Not much statistical data is available regarding interpersonal conflict on the job, but several studies suggest a gradual increase in such problems since 1999. For example, a recent nationwide survey titled Civility in America found that nearly one-third of Americans claim to experience incivility at work.

My own experience tells me that far too many American workers are wasting time dealing with the destructive and inappropriate behavior of others, which hinders their ability to be productive and efficient employees.

In the book *Choosing Civility: The Twenty-Five Rules of Considerate Conduct* by Dr. P.M. Forni, the author and professor at Johns Hopkins University states the following, "There is no doubt in my mind that assertiveness is part of the set of quiet but powerful interactive skills of civility."

Your future career may very well depend on it. People work in teams. In most progressive companies, the days of thinking that someone is a good fit because they're technically sound or competent are pretty much gone. Your ability to maintain positive work relationships is critical to your work success, so much so that it's quite common during job interviews to be asked how you handle conflict or have overcome problems at work.

Today, most companies and hiring personnel strive to hire the right people – those who are good communicators and good problem solvers. This is also why it isn't unusual for a serious workplace conflict to result in the loss of someone's job, or for ongoing workplace problems to prevent someone from advancing.

For several years, I provided career counseling for employees in our company. Many people were frustrated by their inability to move up in the organization, and my job was to help with resumes, interview coaching, networking, and sometimes obtaining feedback.

One young woman came to me with an excellent resume after unsuccessfully attempting to obtain a higher-level position within the organization. She had a master's degree and presented herself very well, yet in spite of more than thirty applications over the past year, she'd garnered no real interest and only a few interviews. I asked about her work history and she insisted that it was very positive, so I offered to do some interviews and to contact people she had previously worked for to see if I could gain insight into what might be problematic. I explained that I would be asking pointed questions to help her and that she needed to be prepared to hear the feedback. She agreed.

When we met for follow-up, I told her that my impression was that she should begin to look outside the organization for a promotion. Based on the feedback I had received from at least three previous supervisors, she had a reputation for being divisive and manipulative, and none of the three could give her a good reference.

I offered her this feedback in a straightforward manner while trying to be supportive. She needed to know this information so that she could work toward a realistic job opportunity instead of continuing to hit a dead end.

Alas, her perspective was that others were threatened by her knowledge and abilities. She wound up leaving the organization, and I can only assume that her problems continued in her new workplace, given the attitude she projected. She didn't seem to understand that knowledge, education, and ability are not always enough for career success. As Tina Seeling points out in her book *What I Wish I Knew When I Was 20*, we live in a small world, and it's quite important that we avoid burning bridges, no matter how tempted we may be to do so. You aren't going to like everyone you meet and not everyone is going to like you, but there's no need to make enemies. In your career, your reputation is your most valuable asset, and it needs to be guarded well. You never know whom you might be working with or for in the future, or whom that person interviewing you for that dream job may know from your past.

Getting along with colleagues lessens the odds of workplace violence. I don't want to be an alarmist, but workplace violence is a real concern, despite the fact that violence caused by interpersonal problems on the job is statistically very rare. The truth is that when it comes to the subject of violence in the workplace, it's not the statistics that people tend to think about but rather the stories or incidents we hear or read about.

Simply put, most of us do not want to put ourselves at further risk by adding to our conflicts with others. It's much better to handle problems in a straightforward and respectful manner so that negative feelings do not escalate.

A related issue is the fear of retribution or retaliation. Repeatedly, employees have told me they are afraid to speak up about a problem with a colleague and even more afraid to address a problem with a superior. Usually employees explain that they "don't want to make the situation worse," but they also at times intimate that they don't want any backlash or negative outcome as a result of discussing a problem.

The fear of retribution or retaliation can even keep managers from addressing behavioral or work performance problems. In the book *How Did That Happen? Holding People Accountable for Results,* authors Roger Connors and Tom Smith list "fear of retribution" as one of the top reasons managers avoid holding employees accountable for performance. This may be one of those fears that tends to be more irrational than rational, but it is real and it does affect people on the job. It's another important reason to be an effective communicator, problem solver, and relationship maintainer.

Maintaining positive work relationships is obviously very important, but it doesn't mean you should try to cope by being a silent victim to a bad boss or a difficult colleague. The answer is to be a good communicator so that when you do have a problem with someone, you can utilize straightforward and considerate communication to get to a resolution.

As a workplace consultant, I see many people who work very hard at difficult, stressful jobs who neither want nor need additional stress from their co-workers, whether bosses or subordinates. Unfortunately, it's not unusual for people to worry about certain individuals they inevitably must deal with during their day or shift.

The good news is that it isn't necessary to feel this vulnerable. There is a better way. To get to that better way, let's take a look at a department and a specific team of colleagues who all have different approaches to workplace conflict and see how their interpersonal challenges play out.

CHAPTER TWO

A WORKPLACE DRAMA DEVELOPS

Paul, Ted, Sally, and Kim work together in the same department. They were all hired at the same time about three years ago. Since then, the department has grown significantly and each of the four has developed a reputation that over time has resulted in their receiving a nickname within the department.

PUSHOVER PAUL

Paul is known as "Pushover Paul." Unfortunately, the name fits him pretty well. Paul's behavior tends to be passive. He is known in the department as the nice, easy-going guy who never says no but also never stands up for himself.

Paul is easily taken advantage of and rarely, if ever, gets what he wants. The nice part is that he doesn't seem to care. Paul always goes with the flow and works to please others and he even lets people know that pleasing others is what makes him happy.

The benefit to being Paul is that he never really has to deal with any conflicts. He just periodically swallows his pride and keeps his mouth shut. The problem is, by smiling and nodding when he doesn't feel like it and agreeing when he really disagrees, Paul is all but guaranteeing that he'll wind up feeling bitter about all of the above at some point in the future.

Over a period of time, Paul will either blow up and rip someone up one side and down the other or he will internalize all his quiet frustration until he's forced to seek medical help for the health issues he's surely going to develop. If the anger doesn't get the best of him, the years of pent-up frustration will lead to either psychological or medical problems he cannot avoid.

This sounds extreme, but let's face reality: people who are always meeting other people's needs and ignoring their own develop a great deal of pent-up frustration, and it has to find release somehow.

Paul takes others' feelings into consideration, but unfortunately not his own. His motto is, "Oh, don't worry about me! As long as you're happy, and you're happy and you're happy and…" Hence, Pushover Paul.

TYRANT TED

Ted's nickname is "Tyrant Ted." According to his colleagues, this fits his personality to a "T." Ted gets what he wants through intimidation, speaking loudly, being pushy, and sometimes just plain being mean. He laughs off the nickname, but deep down he's proud of his "get it done" style.

Ted is an aggressive person. Depending on the situation, he may yell, berate, belittle, stomp, bully, or exhibit any other hostile behavior he feels is necessary. He doesn't care about other people's feelings. His motto is, "Whatever it takes to get my way is just fine, no matter who gets hurt in the process." He can embarrass a colleague or be mean and rude and feel perfectly justified in his behavior.

Ted gets a lot done, but very few people can stand him. Virtually everyone avoids him and describes him in unkind or unflattering terms behind his back. A few people think he's a strong leader, but these are people who have yet to witness or hear about his methods. In fact, these are usually people in higher positions within the company in front of whom Ted would never display such behavior.

The downside for Ted is that eventually his conduct is going to catch up with him. It may take a while, but eventually he'll begin to experience the consequences of his behavior, probably in the form of strained relationships, being labeled a jerk, and being passed over for promotions.

Scheming Sally

Sally's nickname is "Scheming Sally." Because the name is never used in her presence, she has no idea so many of her colleagues mistrust her. Sally is not straightforward. On the contrary, her primary style is passive-aggressive. She will say one thing but often she means something very different. When confronted, Sally doesn't take responsibility. Instead, she runs for cover. She is often friendly to your face, but watch out, my friend.

Sally dislikes direct conflict so she says one thing while really meaning another. She will not tell you directly what she thinks or wants but eventually it comes out through negative body language, tone of voice, sarcastic or so-called "joking" remarks, or by sharing her displeasure with everyone but the source of her concern.

People tend to avoid Sally. She has a reputation for talking under her breath during meetings and for sitting with her arms folded in an angry "I don't want to be here" posture. Afterwards, it's quite common for her to run to colleagues with various complaints.

Sally tries to get her point across by getting others upset. When sharing "stories about others," she frequently uses negative body language and sarcastic comments, but she always denies being a part of any negative behavior or problem. She is quite manipulative and everyone seems to see it except for her. She has few friends because few people can deal with this behavior.

The truth is, anyone can be Sally's victim. She doesn't know how to be upfront so she eventually turns off even those who are close to her. Sally is very frustrating to deal with, but she's also the last to know what's going on. By the time she finds out, it's usually too late.

Scheming Sally wants people to think she considers their feelings, but that's not really the case. It's all about Sally, and while she doesn't understand that, those around her do. Her motto is, "I may not tell you what I think, but you'll figure it out one way or another."

KIM

Kim doesn't really have a nickname in the department, though some people affectionately call her "Kim the Kind-hearted." People not only like Kim but they also respect and trust her. She is a good communicator, she handles problems well, and she avoids getting involved in department gossip or drama. Kim gets along with everyone and is considered a high performer in her work.

Kim's primary style is assertive. She is straightforward but nice. You know where you stand with Kim and you can trust her. She always gets her point across in a respectful manner and she never berates, belittles, or embarrasses people. She is firm when necessary but always in a respectful and caring way.

Kim understands the importance of positive relationships and feels a sense of responsibility for developing and maintaining them. Kim values her work and her reputation very much and she wants to accomplish a great deal. She knows that without positive relationships, work and life itself are much harder. Sure, she occasionally sees people get ahead who lack basic kindness and the ability to communicate effectively, but she knows that how things look and how things actually are can be two very different things. She also knows that negative behaviors and attitudes eventually catch up to people and hurt their reputations.

Most of the people Kim has admired over the years are those with excellent communication skills. These are people who are well liked and respected by the majority of their co-workers. Kim's motto is, "Positive and straightforward communication is the key to good relationships and problem solving."

Interdepartment Conflict

Paul, Ted, Sally, and Kim get along with each other fairly well, but their department is having some difficulties with another department they all work closely with and must rely on. Accusations from each department have been flying back and forth, and both department heads have held special meetings to try to work out the problems. Meanwhile, the complaints keep coming.

Paul, Ted, Sally, and Kim all agree that management needs to do something, as the obvious strain has created some interesting and rather dysfunctional phone calls between the two departments.

While they're in agreement on this issue, the ways in which these four co-workers handle their various challenges differ considerably.

THE ROLE OF INTERPERSONAL STYLES

Paul, Ted, Sally, and Kim have very different approaches to handling conflict, and these approaches are not created equal. As you will see below, they have a significant impact on each co-worker's ability to communicate, resolve conflicts, and do their work.

While it is true that there are times in life when being more passive or aggressive is in our best interests, these tend to be rare occasions. There are also times when each of us behaves in a passive-aggressive manner. We aren't proud of these moments, but such behaviors do slip out occasionally.

But Paul, Ted, and Sally aren't "slipping up." Their styles have become so ingrained that they've developed predictable patterns of behavior. Unfortunately, though their approaches may appear to work in the short term, they are painful in the long run.

As these different styles are presented, think about which one most closely reflects how you handle conflicts and/or differences with others.

PAUL

First, let's return to Paul, who is actually quite a nice guy. Paul believes it's easier to keep his mouth shut and to run from conflict than to address it. There may be some initial payoff for Paul in behaving this way, but the drawbacks are numerous and quite costly. It is hard to have healthy self-esteem and a sense of peace when you cannot express yourself, discuss your concerns, or otherwise meet your needs.

True to form, Paul doesn't say much about the problems he's having. He's been verbally abused by one person from the other department but he figures management will address this at some point. He told his boss what was going on, but nothing changed so Paul is suffering in silence. Nonetheless, he dreads dealing with this person. Day in and day out, he goes to work feeling stressed, and he leaves feeling the same way. He is very frustrated, but he doesn't want to talk to the person he's struggling with for fear of making the situation worse. He also fears the other person won't care anyway. Paul believes the guy is just a jerk, and nothing is likely to change that.

Paul would be much better off physically and mentally if he communicated in a straightforward manner. Being quiet and allowing yourself to be taken advantage of is hard on the body and the spirit, and the stress just builds. Sure enough, Paul is increasingly unhappy, both at work and at home, and the trickle-down effect means his wife isn't very happy, either.

Ted

Ted, of course, isn't afraid of conflict. On the contrary, he frequently creates conflict because he's learned that it's easy to bulldoze others to get what he wants. His needs are not only important but he feels they are worthy of being met at the expense of others. While there may be some short-term payoffs for Ted, the long-term consequences aren't very positive. Suffice it to say, his lack of sensitivity to other people is causing additional problems and damaging his reputation.

Ted has gotten into a few verbal arguments with several people on the other team. At one point, he found himself yelling at one of these colleagues before slamming down the phone in disgust. His supervisor talked to him about it and threatened disciplinary action but Ted explained that his actions were in response to the other person's blatantly rude behavior. His boss reminded him that two wrongs do not make a right and that Ted needs to control himself and act professionally at all times, no matter what behavior is thrown at him.

Not surprisingly, Ted sat fuming while he endured this lecture, determined not to let anyone bully him.

All the same, Ted doesn't want to lose his job, so he decides to confront the behavior as suggested by his boss, who asks him to contact the person he hung up on and apologize. Ted calls up this person and the conversation goes as follows:

TED: Hey Chuck, this is Ted. You mind if I tell you something?

CHUCK: Sure, what's up?

TED: I really did not appreciate how you spoke to me the other day. You do not need to yell at me when I ask a question.

CHUCK: I did not yell. You actually yelled at me.

TED: You've got to be kidding me. I can't believe you won't admit what you did. I guess there's no need to discuss this further.

CHUCK: Guess not. (Slams the phone down.)

This interaction reinforces Ted's belief that it doesn't do any good to talk to people when there's a problem. Chuck is a jerk and always will be. From Ted's perspective, it's always the other person who's the problem.

SALLY

Meanwhile, Sally has been talking to everyone she can find about her frustrations. She's particularly upset about one person in the other department and has been taking copious notes about their discussions. Sally has had several orders delayed and feels it's due to this person's arrogance and incompetence, so she's put together a letter outlining the problems and has asked several colleagues to sign it. She plans to send this memo to her supervisor as well as the other department head.

When Sally's supervisor visits to ask her about the letter everyone is talking about, Sally explains how fed up she is. Her boss asks what she's done to address the issue and Sally replies that she's made her needs very clear. She further explains that her colleague has no interest in doing a good job and that talking to her is useless. She adds that she's surprised the company puts up with such incompetence.

The supervisor explains to Sally that she has a reputation for stirring up trouble in the department and demands that she stop the letter campaign immediately.

Sally folds her arms, sighs, rolls her eyes, and denies any involvement or participation in the complaining, adding that she's just trying to get her job done despite others who hold her back. She denies any knowledge of the letter and mentions another colleague in the department the supervisor might want to talk to about it instead.

Sally has learned that while she can't speak directly to express her needs or concerns, she can still get some needs met by acting out, either behind the scenes or through nonverbal communication. This is easier for her than being direct, but it has earned her a reputation as a backstabber, a manipulator, and as someone who is totally untrustworthy. Her approach simply makes situations and relationships more difficult for herself and for those who work with her.

Kim

Then there's Kim. She has joked with a few people from the other department about some of their problems and gets along with most of them. She recognizes that a lot of the issues she's encountering are process problems that need to be worked out and she understands that leadership is addressing them, though it seems to be taking forever.

Unfortunately, Kim has been treated very poorly by a particular member of the other team and is really bothered by it. She doesn't understand where it's coming from. She realizes there are issues on both sides, but she's curious about why the conversation is strained and difficult every time she has to talk with this person.

Just the other day, Kim had to call in an order and this individual responded with her usual short, terse answers. Every time Kim asked a question, her co-worker replied, "I don't know." It didn't matter what the question was, because at one point Kim asked this person how her day was going and received the same apathetic "I don't know."

Kim decides she doesn't want this type of relationship to continue, even on the phone. She has to talk with Stacey on a regular basis, and things have deteriorated to the point that she becomes anxious as soon as she hears Stacey's voice.

Kim is simply considerate. She knows that if she were doing something that caused a problem, she would want to know about it. She affords this same consideration to others and recognizes that with a few minutes of thought and a strategy, she can deal with any problem thrown her way. She also understands that the effort she puts into communicating with others has significant benefits. She wishes to be successful in her work, she wants to be respected, and she doesn't want to be burdened with the stress and strain of interpersonal conflicts. Her confidence in her ability to communicate well goes a long way toward creating a sense of peace at work as well as in her personal life.

Not surprisingly, Kim decides to address the legitimate workplace conflict she is experiencing. Equally unsurprising, she is successful. The next chapter explains her approach.

CHAPTER THREE

GSSC, A FOUR PART TECHNIQUE FOR HANDLING INTERPERSONAL CONFLICTS

Handling conflicts at work is an art rather than a science, yet good communicators understand that they are more likely to resolve a problem if they take respectful action than if they wait, hope, or pray something will come along to make it magically disappear. They also know that a focus on resolving whatever problem seems to exist will help guide them in what may be an awkward or uncomfortable conversation.

You'll notice in the cases of Paul, Ted, and Sally that they allow their frustrations and/or anger to get the best of them. Paul avoids the problem and suffers in silence, Ted tries to bulldoze the problem away, and Sally attempts to rally others in eliminating her newfound enemy colleague.

On the other hand, Kim understands that maintaining positive work relationships is important for job success. She also reminds herself that when other people are difficult to deal with, it's often because they are clueless about how they come across. Even when they realize they are being difficult, they certainly do not see the situation from her perspective. Finally, Kim realizes that if she wishes to alter the relationship she has with the woman in the other department, it's up to her to set the wheels in motion.

Kim decides to talk to Stacey, her unfriendly colleague in another department, to find out what can be done to resolve the issue. She doesn't want to let negative feelings build to the point that her stress becomes debilitating. She also wants to improve her relationship with Stacey because she sees the bigger picture.

Kim uses a four-part technique I've termed GSSC to handle this uncomfortable interpersonal conflict. The "G" stands for "Goal," the first "S" stands for "Safe," the second "S" stands for "Share," and the "C" stands for "Clarify."

Before we see how Kim uses the technique, let's take a closer look at these four key steps that can make any conversation a little easier.

GSSC TECHNIQUE FOR HANDLING INTERPERSONAL CONFLICTS

STEP ONE:
IDENTIFY YOUR GOAL (G)

STEP TWO:
MAKE IT SAFE FOR THE OTHER PERSON TO LISTEN TO YOU (S)

STEP THREE:
SHARE YOUR OBSERVATIONS, PERCEPTIONS, OR FEELINGS (IN OTHER WORDS, DO NOT ACCUSE) (S)

STEP FOUR:
CLARIFY AND ASK FOR AN AGREEMENT MOVING FORWARD (C)

ASK QUESTIONS WHILE FOCUSING ON YOUR GOAL

STEP ONE:
IDENTIFY YOUR GOAL (G)

This step is absolutely critical! Identifying your goal makes the upcoming conversation much easier. If you skip this step, everything that follows can be more challenging. Failing to identify your goal also makes you more vulnerable to having the conversation manipulated, getting sidetracked, losing your focus on what's important, wasting time and energy, and ending the conversation poorly.

Your goal can be defined as what you specifically want to accomplish during the conversation. The specific problem may change but the overall goal – maintaining a positive relationship and solving a problem moving forward – does not.

Of course, your goal will vary a bit depending on where you are in your relationship with the person you're having the conflict with. Is this one of your first conversations, or is it later in the process?

More often than not, the goal of your first conversation is to find out if the other person has any awareness of the situation and whether there is a willingness to work with you to improve the situation.

Here are some examples of reasonable goals:

- You want to determine if the person has any awareness of the problem and/or cares enough to help.

- You want to find out what the person is willing to do to resolve the problem.
- You want to find out if the person will agree to stop or start a certain behavior.

Before beginning a conversation, make sure you are clear about what you want. Identifying your goal up front is critical.

Kim has identified her goal: to improve her relationship with Stacey so that necessary phone calls no longer create stress and tension. She's almost ready to initiate the conversation, but before she does, she also needs to take some time to think about how best to begin this conversation. A successful phone call requires that she keep step two in mind: making it safe for Stacey to listen.

STEP TWO:
MAKE IT SAFE FOR THE OTHER PERSON TO LISTEN TO YOU (S)

Before approaching Stacey, Kim remembers that timing and privacy are critical for any important discussion. She knows that talking to someone in the heat of the moment isn't wise. Neither is talking to someone in an open area where other people can overhear or observe the conversation. This may sound like basic common sense, but it's ignored all too frequently.

Kim also remembers to think before she speaks. When I give presentations on assertive communication, people often say they can't think quickly enough to give a good response to people they are having a conflict with. This is an interesting perspective, because the truth is that we're often better off saying nothing until we've had some time to reflect and truly think about what it is that's bothering us and what we want to do about it. Heat-of-the-moment discussions often do not lead to positive outcomes and they may do serious damage to all involved.

> *The best time to have a discussion is after you've had a little time to think about the situation and have privacy for the discussion.*

Begin difficult conversations by making it safe to hear you as opposed to jumping right into the problem. If you want people to be willing to listen to you, you need to make it safe for them to do so. If you open with something that reflects your true intentions, it makes it a lot easier for the other person to actually hear what you have to say.

Yet all too often, like Tyrant Ted when he approached his co-worker Chuck, people begin with an accusation or an attitude that says, "Let me tell you what your problem is," and then they wonder why the person is resistant to hearing feedback.

Think about why it is that we give feedback. We give it because we want to help resolve a problem, we want the other person to do better, or we want to enhance our relationship with another person. These are all positive and caring reasons. If we didn't care about this person or need to work collaboratively in some way, we wouldn't bother to initiate a conversation.

Here are some examples of how to open a conversation safely:

- You and I have worked together for a while now, and I want to make sure that we are always supportive of each other.
- You know that I enjoy working with you and want us to trust each other.
- My intention is for us to resolve a problem, and I need your help.
- I really want your help with something, and I would appreciate hearing your perspective too.
- You know how much I appreciate all your help and support. I'm struggling with something, and I want to find out what we can do to improve it.

Start the conversation by making it safe for the other person to listen. This means letting this person know your positive intention to problem-solve rather than to make accusations.

Kim does a masterful job of beginning with a goal in mind while making it safe for Stacey to listen. She also calls during a quiet time when there is no business to discuss. Here's how the conversation begins, with my comments about pertinent parts of the conversation in italics:

Kim: Hi Stacey. It's Kim from Satellite 9. How are you today?

Stacey: What do you need?

Stacy is her usual terse and unpleasant self, but Kim stays focused on her goal and does not let Stacy's tone of voice influence her own attitude. She realizes her first step in having a successful conversation with Stacy is making it safe for her to listen.

Kim: Well, I actually do not need anything at the moment. I wanted to talk to you if I could, just for a few minutes. Would now be a good time for you?

Stacey: Go ahead.

Kim: Well, we've been working together over the phone now for several weeks, and it's important to me that we have a good working relationship. Our work is connected now, and I want us to both feel positive about our interactions. I just wanted to share my perspective with you and see what your thoughts are on this issue. Would you mind?

Kim chooses her words thoughtfully, keeping her goal in mind.

Stacey: I'm not aware of any problems.

Kim: Well, that's good to hear. When I contact you for an order, I sometimes feel that you may be upset or that you are bothered by my call, and I just wanted to make sure that there isn't a problem.

STACEY: I don't have a problem with you or your calls. What makes you think that?

This is a tricky moment for Kim, but as you will soon see, she handles it masterfully. She knows that when confronting problems with others, it is best to keep in mind the third key step in the communication process: share your observations, perceptions, or feelings but do not make accusations.

> *Avoid making accusations while you share your observations, perceptions, or feelings. You are not looking for a confession; you are trying to problem-solve and move forward.*

STEP THREE:
SHARE YOUR OBSERVATIONS,
PERCEPTIONS, OR FEELINGS (S)

How do you go about sharing your perspective with a colleague when you are hoping to change something in your work relationship? Whatever is easiest for you and fits your personality best will do. The key point is to avoid the blame game.

Too often, people begin with accusations or leap straight to the problem only to find the other person defensive or argumentative. There's a big difference between stating "You came back from break ten minutes late" and "It appeared as though you didn't return from break until ten minutes late."

Not surprisingly, this is where people often trip up. When we share our thoughts, we naturally like it when others agree with us. Just remember your goal. It isn't to have the person admit failures or mistakes, own up to their behaviors, or acknowledge how brilliant you are for noticing their shortcomings. You are simply trying to solve a problem moving forward. You want to move on from here, so there's no value in arguing over what really happened. You don't need to care about that. You just want to solve the problem moving forward.

> *If you begin a conversation expecting to hear a confession, you will usually wind up quite disappointed.*

Examples of how you might share your perspective or observations include the following:

- I wanted to share my perspective on something with you.
- I have a concern about something that happened yesterday morning and I want to share my observation.
- Something happened yesterday, and I want to share what I observed and see what was going on from your viewpoint.

- I'm not sure if you were aware of this, but yesterday I noticed…
- I felt that…and as a result I was thinking…

But sometimes, like Kim, you just have to feel your way through the problem. Though Stacey isn't particularly forthcoming, Kim remembers to keep her focus on problem-solving for the future as the conversation continues and she shares her perspective with Stacey:

KIM: Sometimes I feel it's your tone of voice. Sometimes it seems very short and tense from my perspective, as if you aren't happy with my call. I just wanted to know if there was any problem on my end? The other day when I said "Thanks and have a good day," I thought you responded with "Whatever." It made me feel that you were angry or upset. I just want to make sure that you are okay with me and to find out if there is anything I can do differently.

Kim avoids accusing Stacey as she shares her feelings and perceptions.

STACEY: No, not at all. I'm not sure what you are talking about, and I can't believe I used "Whatever." Just let me know if I sound like I'm having a problem.

Kim recognizes that whether or not Stacey uses the word "Whatever" is not the issue. Who cares? Kim just wants to problem-solve moving forward, and she understands the importance of the fourth and last key step in communicating to resolve conflicts: clarify what you both heard and ask for an agreement moving forward.

STEP FOUR:
CLARIFY AND ASK FOR AN AGREEMENT MOVING FORWARD (C)

Do you ever have conversations that end with you wondering how the other person heard something totally different from what you said? If your answer is no, you must be a great communicator. Because this does happen to most people at some time or another, it's important to make sure both participants hear the same thing. You accomplish this by repeating what you've heard. Restate the conclusion you think you have come to and check to be sure the other person agrees. Then make sure you end with an agreement moving forward by asking what you should do if the problem reoccurs.

> *Don't assume you are on the same page as a colleague or boss at the end of a problem-solving conversation, even when it seems to go well. Instead, clarify what you both heard and ask for an agreement moving forward.*

Good communicators recognize that people are creatures of habit who sometimes fall into bad habits with little awareness. Most of the time, one conversation does not make an issue disappear. The truth is, if you want someone to work on changing a behavior, you're going to have to remind them of this behavior or somehow help them remember it in the future.

Nonetheless, since most people want to know if there's a problem or something they're doing that's bothersome, they will most likely say something to the effect of, "Please let me know if it happens again."

If they don't, what they do say will certainly be interesting and may give you additional insight that will be helpful to you.

Examples of how to end a conversation by clarifying what was shared and coming to an agreement moving forward include the following:

- Great. So we agree that you'll ask me if I need help once you complete your assignment, and I'll do the same for you. Is that correct? Okay, now what if either of us seems to forget this and there's another problem?
- Okay, this is what I understand. You will let me know when you need to leave and will double-check to make sure I can handle things by myself. If I can't, you will postpone leaving until I have things under control. Is that correct? Great. What should I do if there appears to be a problem again?
- So you agree that you will try to be more aware of your tone of voice when we discuss a future problem. If I notice it happening again, do you want me to let you know?

Here is how Kim handles the critical fourth step of clarifying and coming to an agreement:

KIM: Thank you. That sounds like a good plan. We need to talk regularly, and I just want to make sure there isn't any problem. So my understanding is that you have no problem working with me. If I call again and feel the same concern, I can bring it up next time?

Kim pleasantly clarifies and restates the agreement she believes she and Stacy have come to in order to be sure they are on the same page.

STACEY: Sure. Whatever.

The fact is, how you develop your agreement moving forward isn't as important as just doing it. People often complain that trying to resolve problems with other people isn't worth the time and effort because things get better for a little while and then they revert back to where they were, but that's just human nature. Most of us fall back into old habits quite easily, and behavior changes aren't easily sustained without some help.

Stacey's final "Whatever" is a case in point, but if we could just cut others a break and be happy that they're trying to work with us, we'd be more open to thoughtfully reinforcing the agreement. They've already agreed to work it out, so what's wrong with kindly approaching them again as they've already agreed to? If they push back, you can always remind them that they told you to let them know if the problem reoccurred.

> *People tend to be creatures of habit. We often do things without being completely aware. This makes behavior change difficult, which is why the help of others is so important.*

By talking with Stacey, Kim has taken control of the problem. She never accuses Stacy of anything and she stays focused on her goal throughout the discussion. As a result, Stacey is more aware of how she is being perceived and she understands Kim's desire to work well together. If Stacey continues her troubling behavior on the phone or if it resumes, she has given Kim permission to mention it again. If the problem continues in spite of Kim's attempt to address it, Kim can always ask for help from a supervisor. Hopefully it won't come to this, but at least Kim has given Stacey the benefit of the doubt and attempted to work it out with her directly.

CHAPTER FOUR

ASKING QUESTIONS, YOUR SAFETY NET WHEN RESOLVING CONFLICTS

One of the most significant reasons people fail to talk to others when there's a problem is the fear of how that person will react. This uncertainty leads to some of those irrational beliefs I mentioned earlier, thoughts such as "It'll just make things worse" or "He already knows and just doesn't care, so why bother?"

The fact is, when conversations don't go well, it's usually because the person initiating the conversation doesn't approach it in the best manner. If you come across too aggressively, too passively, or even passive-aggressively, or if you proceed without keeping your goal in mind, the odds for a positive outcome are diminished. You might then blame the other individual for not seeing the light and for displaying a lack of personal accountability. After that, you might try even harder to avoid further discussions.

A simple way to remove any fear you may have about participating in a conversation about a workplace problem is to ask questions. This is a great but underappreciated communication technique.

Asking questions is actually your secret weapon in communication because it can provide great insight into how to solve your problem. Just remember to stay focused on your goal of solving a problem instead of looking for a confession or recognition of how right you are.

When someone says something to you that you aren't sure of, you don't understand, you can't believe they said, or something that makes you nervous, come back with a question. For example:

- I'm sorry; can you explain what you mean by that?
- Are you saying that you work harder than everyone else in the department or did I misunderstand you? Why do you feel this way?
- Would you agree that it's important that we cover for each other when we're on break?
- Are you saying that there's no way the two of us can work this problem out?
- Are you suggesting my only option to resolve this is to get management involved?
- Is there anything that would make this better for you or that would allow you to consider my perspective?

Questions are important because they help clarify what you heard. They give people a chance to explain themselves while providing further insight into what they're thinking. Questions also help you get back to your goal when you need to refocus.

See how Kim utilizes this safety net when Stacey throws her a curve ball at the end of their conversation by adding the following comment:

STACEY: You know, you seem rather bossy to me.

This statement doesn't throw Kim because she is still focused on her goal. Also, she knows how to stay focused on coming to a resolution by employing the safety net of asking questions.

KIM: How do I seem bossy to you?

STACEY: Well, I don't know. You just seem bossy to me. That's all.

KIM: You can't explain how or in what way?

STACEY: No. It's just a feeling I get.

KIM: You do understand that I'm just trying to figure out a way that we can work better together, don't you?

Kim goes back to the main goal.

STACEY: Yeah, I guess so.

KIM: I just want to make sure that we can have positive communication between us when we need to work together, and I appreciate your help, Stacey. Thanks again, and I'll talk to you soon.

Kim stays totally focused on her main goal by restating it before pleasantly ending the conversation.

STACEY: Fine. Goodbye.

Kim asks Stacey about her statement but doesn't get caught up in it or let it detract from what she is attempting to do. She has already accepted the fact that Stacey isn't the easiest person to deal with and certainly isn't someone she wants to hang out with, but she accepts that has to work with her. Kim's goal is to decrease the stress she feels when she talks to Stacy, and she is well on her way to achieving her goal because of the conversation she initiated.

Sam and Frank in the example below offer another and more extreme example that illustrates the benefits of incorporating questions into a difficult conversation.

Throughout the conversation, as needed, ask questions to help you stay focused on the goal and to problem-solve.

Sam works closely with Frank. He finds this to be a challenge because Frank spends a lot of time walking around, wasting time, and complaining to others. The irony is that Frank often grumbles about all the work he has to do and the fact that he works harder than anyone else.

Most of the people Frank works with seem to feel he's one of those sitcom personalities, the person who bugs the heck out of everyone but is so obnoxious that their co-workers just shake their heads in disbelief. Most of us think these characters are funny, but only when we don't have to deal with them.

Because Frank has begun coming to him more and more frequently with his complaints, Sam, who has an assertive style, decides to talk to him about it. Before he begins, he identifies his goal. After thinking about it, Sam decides he wants to find out if Frank has any awareness of how he complains about his work and whether or not he's willing to stop that behavior, at least around Sam. Having identified his goal, here's how the conversation goes:

SAM: Thanks for talking to me, Frank. I appreciate it. I'm having a problem with something and I wanted to ask you about it and see what we can do to get past it.

Sam starts the conversation with step two, by making it safe for Frank to listen.

FRANK: Is this something about me?

SAM: Well, it has to do with you and me. You see, I really like my work a great deal and I like the people I work with very much. My perspective is that work is difficult at times and it's important to me to keep a positive attitude. There are times when you may not realize it, but you sometimes seem to say negative things about this place and some of the people.

Sam stays focused on his goal and employs step three, sharing his perspective and observation instead of attacking and accusing.

FRANK: Well, I work very hard here and I often feel that I do more work than anyone else, including you.

SAM: So, you feel that you do more work than I do and that's why you are so negative. Is that correct?

Sam asks questions to better understand.

FRANK: I carry the heaviest load here and everyone knows it. It's hard to be positive when you feel that others are having an easy time of it, while you are constantly badgered about getting things done. I run around here like a chicken with my head cut off half the time. Don't you see that?

SAM: Frank, I'm sorry you feel that way, but however you may feel, I really would appreciate it if you could help me with the negative comments. If you could just agree to avoid making negative statements or complaints about work or others while around me, I would really appreciate that.

Sam stays focused on his goal and avoids getting distracted by what he sees as Frank's unrelated and totally ridiculous comments.

FRANK: Well, I'll see what I can do, but I can't make any promises.

SAM: So you will work to avoid negative comments around me?

Sam continues the conversation with step four, seeking to clarify his understanding and ask for an agreement moving forward; he does this by asking a question.

FRANK: I'll try, but it won't be easy.

SAM: I appreciate your making the effort. I know it's not easy, but I'll try to help by pointing it out to you if it happens again. Okay?

FRANK: Well, for goodness sake, let me know. I can't keep track of what I'm talking about half the time.

Sam handles this challenging conversation very well. First, he focuses on what he can address – Frank's behavior in his presence. He knows he can't solve the problem for the department, but at least he can address what occurs in front of him.

Second, while he may be totally blown away by Frank's accusation that he, Frank, works harder than Sam, Sam remains focused on his goal. He stays on track by asking Frank a pivotal question: "You are saying that you do more work than anyone and that's why you are so negative?"

Frank's response doesn't matter as much as how Sam follows up. He acknowledges Frank's frustration but comes right back to the main goal. He now knows that Frank has some awareness of what he's doing even if his reasons are crazy.

Sam also maintains his self-control throughout this conversation and doesn't react when Frank says he works harder than Sam. Who cares? Sam just wants the negativity to stop and he succeeds in getting Frank to say that he will try.

Sam is realistic. He knows what he is dealing with in Frank. They will never be friends, but Sam needs to be able to function around him at work. His goal is to decrease Frank's negativity and he is well on his way to achieving it.

Staying focused on what is truly important is the key. Sam accomplishes this by addressing the immediate problem and doing his best to put a stop to it moving forward. He isn't worried about how obnoxious Frank is overall and he doesn't care about what has happened thus far. He just wants to solve the problem moving forward. He's made Frank aware, and the next time Frank starts talking negatively in Sam's presence, Sam will quickly remind him of their agreement. After a few reminders, Frank will probably remember that he needs to find another place to vent.

The same is true for Kim. Inside, she considers Stacey to be a real piece of work and she wonders how she was ever hired in the first place. Despite this, Kim chooses to focus on what is important: how her interactions with Stacey proceed moving forward. She wants the stress and tension she feels every time she calls Stacey to stop.

Thanks to how well Kim stays focused and her ability to avoid being sidetracked in the conversation, the odds are very good that Stacey will change her behavior on the phone with Kim. If she doesn't, she knows Kim will address it. Since Kim has an assertive style, she'll be sure to pursue the problem if it continues. If and when Kim goes to the boss with a continued and documented concern about Stacey's behavior, her boss will be more inclined to address the situation. After all, Kim has already done her best to talk with Stacey directly about the problem.

As it turns out, Kim's discussion with Stacey proves to be very beneficial. The next time they talk about a work order, Stacey has changed her tone and actually makes a joke. As time goes by, she even tries bonding with Kim by telling her stories about people in Kim's department. A specific target seems to be Ted, but Kim remains quiet and doesn't participate in any gossip with Stacey. She politely repeats that she gets along fine with Ted and then changes the topic. Kim values her reputation and doesn't want to get dragged into the "rumor mill" that seems so easy for others to participate in.

A few months down the road, when Stacey answers the phone sounding irritated, Kim immediately asks if she is okay. When Stacey says she is fine, her tone is much more positive. Thanks to their conversation, Kim's question reminds Stacey to be more aware of the attitude she is projecting toward others since she's not always naturally very self-aware. In the event that Stacey continued to be negative on the phone, Kim can always remind her of their past conversation and her desire to continue their positive interactions.

CHAPTER FIVE

THE WORKPLACE DRAMA GETS MORE COMPLICATED

For a time, relations improve between the two departments but then the bad news descends like a nightmare: Paul, Ted, Sally, and Kim learn that their supervisor, Ed, is being promoted while another supervisor, Diane, who has the reputation of being very difficult to work with, is taking over their department in addition to continuing to run her current department.

Paul feels very threatened and is worried about what difficult behavior he'll be subjected to now.

Ted, though worried, knows that no one will be able to mess with him. He's worked for poor leaders before and he tells his colleagues that he'll just be out of here if the boss is too difficult. He likes to bring up the fact that he can get a job anywhere, although he's been in the same department for over fifteen years.

Initially, Sally is excited because she never liked Ed anyway. He once had the gall to accuse her of being manipulative. A new supervisor means new opportunities.

Kim is the most upset by the news. She knows how important it is to have a great supervisor and she's very worried about the dramatic changes about to take place. Despite her concerns, she is confident in her abilities and knows she can deal with whatever lies ahead.

Things progress fairly well during the transitional months of the restructuring period, but when the department begins to see less of Ed and more of Diane, morale plummets. Diane runs staff meetings as if she were an angry schoolmaster and the team her problematic students. She makes the agenda, she controls the discussions, and she frequently interrupts others. It doesn't take long for her to earn an unflattering reputation.

During one meeting, she cuts an employee off in mid-sentence and tells him that perhaps he should be better prepared before speaking in meetings. No one besides Diane speaks for the remainder of the meeting.

Paul, Ted, Sally, and Kim are not immune to the challenges their new supervisor brings.

At Paul's performance evaluation, which has always been fairly positive, the supervisor tells him his productivity is unsatisfactory and she questions whether this job is actually a good fit for him.

Paul responds that he likes his job and will do whatever is necessary to improve. The supervisor tells him he has two months to turn things around or he will be placed on notice. Paul leaves the meeting crushed, hoping to improve his performance, but fearing the worst. He decides to update his resume and begin looking for another job, just in case.

Sally's relationship with the supervisor is different. She and Diane hit it off immediately over their shared love of reality TV. They get along just fine until Sally shows up late for a regular staff meeting and the supervisor stops in the middle of her speech to sarcastically thank Sally for arriving late.

All eyes are on Sally, who spends the rest of the meeting with her arms folded, angrily glaring at the supervisor, while the other members of the department silently remind themselves to always be on time. Sally leaves the meeting determined to only do the bare minimum in her job from now on. She also begins a campaign of undermining Diane with anyone who will listen.

Though he isn't a big fan of Sally's, Ted decides he's had enough of the supervisor's inappropriate behavior. He isn't going to be treated like a child nor is he going to be embarrassed or humiliated like the others. He decides to have a discussion with Diane, and this is how it goes:

TED: Thanks for meeting with me. I needed to talk to you because of some issues our department is struggling with recently. I realize that you are new to the department and you may not be aware of how we've worked together for some time. Perhaps if I shared some of that information with you, it would help you and our team.

SUPERVISOR: I have no interest in hearing about the past.

TED: I understand that you are not interested in what has worked here previously. I'm just trying to share some feedback with you that I think would be helpful.

SUPERVISOR: Go on.

TED: The staff feels that you do not listen to them. There are times we feel that we're being treated like children and you are the disapproving parent.

SUPERVISOR: Is it you who feels this way or are you here to represent the team?

TED: Both. I feel this way and so does the majority of the team.

SUPERVISOR: Well, I'm very sorry that you and the team feel this way. I appreciate you bringing this to my attention. (Gets up from the chair and walks toward the door.) I'll certainly consider your concerns and hopefully you and the team will feel that your concerns were heard.

TED: I really appreciate your time and your concern. Thanks so much.

Ted leaves feeling great about talking to the boss and setting the record straight. He is convinced this will not only help him but also the whole department.

Several days later, another staff meeting is held. From Ted's perspective, it's brutal. He feels like Diane attacked him, and the rest of the team is clearly uncomfortable at what they witness, too.

Afterwards, Ted tries to figure out where he went wrong. He is normally very aggressive, but he'd toned it down to talk with the new boss. What happened? He'd thought their discussion was a success, but apparently he was wrong. He'd tried to have a reasonable conversation, but Diane hadn't listened. His only choice now, Ted decides, is to go over her head and complain to her boss. That might help, unless it backfires.

Even Kim encounters difficulties with the new supervisor. At one meeting, Kim makes a brief presentation on a project she is heading up. During the presentation, the supervisor cuts Kim off in mid-sentence and tells her that her time is up.

Kim looks at Diane in disbelief and explains that she was told she had ten minutes but that only five have passed.

The supervisor states that Kim should be more aware of the time and that she should hurry up and finish.

Kim, obviously shaken by the rude interruption, cuts her presentation short and ends by asking if anyone has any questions. The rest of the team looks sheepish and no one raises a hand. More than one colleague is thinking, "If Kim gets treated like this, the supervisor is capable of anything."

As the fear level shoots up in the room, Kim returns to her seat, careful to remain calm and to avoid making eye contact with anyone for fear of projecting more anger in the moment.

After the meeting, Kim retreats to her cubicle to think about what happened, what is bothering her the most, and what she can do about it. Although she is angry, Kim realizes she needs to figure out how to work with her supervisor if she wants to stay with the company. She could apply for a job elsewhere, but difficult people work in every company. Who's to say she wouldn't wind up working for someone even more challenging than Diane? Besides, Kim has significant career goals. She wants to stay with this company and move into a higher-level position at some point.

After carefully thinking it over, Kim decides to talk to her supervisor. Because Kim is a good communicator, before she does so, she asks herself the key question: what is my goal?

Kim wants to have a decent relationship with her supervisor. She doesn't want to hang out with her after work, but she does want to have a good working relationship. Not only is this important for her career but she doesn't need any additional stress right now. With two small children, a sick parent, and a job filled with stress, she needs to avoid adding to the package.

Kim decides to let her supervisor know how she felt during the presentation interruption and to find out what can be done to prevent something like this from happening again. Unlike Ted, she views this as a discussion to benefit herself rather than the department. While she doesn't like to see so many of her team members unhappy, she understands that such interpersonal problems need to be handled individually.

The next day, Kim passes her supervisor in the hallway and stops and asks if she can set up a meeting.

Diane answers, "Just tell me what you want right now."

Kim understands the importance of good timing and privacy so she tells her supervisor, "I would really appreciate the opportunity to schedule a time for us to meet."

Diane says, "Look, whatever you have to say to me, you can say right now. What's up?"

Kim responds, "Is it not possible to set up a meeting for us to talk?"

The supervisor replies, "Of course not. Call my assistant and get on my calendar. Have a good day."

She walks off, leaving Kim gaping in amazement, wondering how such a rude person came to be in a supervisory position in the first place. Kim doesn't waste much time on this thinking, though. Her efforts are better spent coming up with a strategy for dealing with her supervisor.

Kim is also proud that she didn't give in to having the discussion in the hallway. Communicating successfully with Diane requires advance preparation, and Kim isn't ready. She also realizes it isn't wise to hold this conversation where others might overhear it or interrupt them.

At the scheduled meeting time, Kim sits at her supervisor's desk, ready to initiate the conversation. Here's how it goes:

KIM: I want to thank you for taking the time to talk to me. I've been in the company for several years and it's important to me to do a good job. I have not had a chance to talk with you much, but I want you to know that I really want to have a good working relationship with you. I'm having a problem with something that I need your help with.

Kim starts off by making it safe for her supervisor to listen.

SUPERVISOR: Cut to the chase. What do you want?

KIM: I want to ask you about my presentation yesterday. I felt very upset and blind-sided by being cut off, and I just want to prevent that from happening in the future.

Kim speaks directly and pleasantly, staying focused on her goal.

SUPERVISOR: Well, then, next time make sure you stay on time.

KIM: I thought I did. I was told I had ten minutes on the agenda. I know that I began at 11:00 sharp because I'm always very sensitive about the time I have. It was only about five minutes into the presentation when I was stopped. I didn't have enough time to finish.

Kim explains her perspective while staying focused on her goal; she avoids making any accusations.

SUPERVISOR: Are you accusing me of lying about your time?

KIM: Not at all. I just felt so bad about how things went yesterday, and I'd like to know how it could be prevented in the future.

Again, Kim stays focused on her goal.

SUPERVISOR: Like I said before. Make sure you are on time.

KIM: Just so I understand, are you saying there is nothing I can do differently to avoid being cut off during a presentation?

Kim asks a question to clarify, keeping her voice calm and respectful.

SUPERVISOR: If you are on time, there is no need to worry.

KIM: Well, what if I confirm the time I have right at the beginning of the presentation? Will that work, because then we'll be on the same page?

Kim asks follow-up questions that continue to focus on solving the problem.

SUPERVISOR: That might help.

KIM: Is there anything else you think I can do to improve our working relationship and our communication from your perspective?

Again, Kim asks questions, seeking to have a better understanding of what she is dealing with.

SUPERVISOR: Just be more effective, Kim.

KIM: Can you explain exactly what you are looking for, Diane?

Kim isn't thrown by this statement because she is always prepared to ask questions to try to better understand where another person is coming from.

SUPERVISOR: I just want the key points from now on and the quicker they are delivered, the better it is for me and for you.

KIM: Okay, so how about if, from now on, I double-check on the presentation with you beforehand and make sure I actually take less time than is planned for?

SUPERVISOR: That is excellent.

KIM: Anything else you think I need to do?

SUPERVISOR: No. You actually are one of the strongest performers in this department. Just watch how you present. That will make you even stronger in my book.

KIM: Okay, I understand that you like the shortest version possible and that I should focus on the key points. From now on when I'm on the agenda, I'll double-check with you on the presentation and the time. I'll also make sure that if I have ten minutes, I'll work to be even quicker. Is this what you prefer, just to clarify?

SUPERVISOR: Sounds right to me.

KIM: I appreciate your time and your insight. Thank you very much, and one last question: if you identify any other things I can do to be stronger in my work, would you let me know?

SUPERVISOR: Will do.

Kim is very effective in this difficult conversation with her supervisor. First, she is clear about her goal before initiating the conversation and she stays focused on her goal throughout the discussion, no matter where the supervisor goes or what she brings up.

Second, Kim is careful to share her perspective and observations. She never accuses the supervisor of anything. She simply shares her perceptions and how she feels in a polite but direct manner.

Third, no matter what Diane says in response, Kim is prepared with a non-inflammatory comeback. She simply asks a question and lets her supervisor respond. Asking clarifying questions is Kim's secret weapon, and this technique works because it's so simple and yet so powerful.

Finally, at the end of the meeting, Kim seeks to clarify understanding and asks for an agreement moving forward. She takes a critical step in asking if Diane will give her feedback in the future. She realizes her supervisor is going to be difficult to work with and that she might very well not give her feedback directly but might instead embarrass her in a meeting.

On the other hand, Kim also knows that, moving forward, there is now a good chance the supervisor will be more open and direct with her. Either way, Kim has managed to tell her supervisor how she feels without making a direct attack or accusation. She now has a better understanding of what she is dealing with and she knows how to prevent a reoccurrence of the presentation nightmare she recently experienced.

One additional point to note is that Kim also ignores the fact that her boss doesn't make much sense and is also quite rude. Some people might have a hard time ignoring this, but Kim already knows her boss is difficult and makes little sense. Why should she belabor the point and make things even harder for herself?

Remember that you are focusing on solving a problem for the future. What happened in the past is not important at this point.

Just problem–solve for the future.

Kim's goal is to avoid being cut off during her presentations.

She has figured out what to do to achieve that, and that's all she needs right now. She knows she's not going to change her boss, make her a nicer and more reasonable person, or stop her from causing her colleagues a lot of additional stress. Kim's a grounded realist with good communication skills, and this makes things at work much easier for her. She takes problems at face value and works to resolve them moving forward.

THE WORKPLACE DRAMA ENDS WELL, BUT ONLY FOR ONE

Diane supervised the new department for about ten months before upper management decided she wasn't working out. What Paul, Ted, Sally, and Kim didn't realize when the change was implemented was that Diane was a suspected problem for at least one person in upper management. To help come to a resolution about Diane, she was given additional responsibilities and asked to report to the director, Ed, in order to closely assess her strengths and weaknesses.

Sure enough, these additional responsibilities revealed that Diane's poor management and communication skills were not limited to one area. In fact, so many problems developed and so many complaints poured in that Diane was offered a separation package. This opened up a new supervisory position, which Ted, Sally, and Kim each expressed interest in.

Paul, not surprisingly, declined to apply – he was too afraid of the interview process and he assumed he wouldn't be considered anyway. Besides, he had recently developed a nervous tick due to job stress. The last thing he needed was additional pressure.

Ed told Tyrant Ted he could go through the interview process but that he needed to be aware that his inability to deal with problems effectively would be a major concern. Ted withdrew his application and decided to look for another job.

Sally was told she wouldn't be considered because of several documented complaints from colleagues regarding her behavior. Ed added that recent discussions with Sally showed no recognition of personal accountability. He also mentioned the negative nonverbal communication she frequently exhibited during staff meetings.

Sally didn't say much during this meeting, but she did tell her boss that she appreciated his honesty. As soon as she left the room, she confronted her colleagues to see who had complained about her. Not one colleague was honest with Sally because no one wanted to get on her bad side. On the contrary, they told her they couldn't believe how she'd been treated.

Sally told them she was getting an attorney and is suing since her boss had just lied about the feedback he'd received. Her colleagues just laughed it off since this is a common threat. Besides, little did Sally know that her boss had plenty of documentation of numerous complaints received about her behavior over the years.

Kim was not only encouraged to apply for the job but Ed even told her how valuable she was to the department and the company. He added that not only did she do a good job but she also had something "unique." He wasn't sure what "it" was, but Kim was obviously a special person, someone others looked to for advice and help. She was an informal leader without the title, but the title would soon be hers.

The nice thing about Kim's upcoming promotion is that she will now have even more influence over helping to create a positive work environment. After all, most people want to come to work and work in peace. Creating this environment is important to Kim, and she takes responsibility for making it a reality. Whatever problems come her way, she feels a sense of confidence that she can find a solution. She recognizes that there is plenty of stress at work already and she doesn't want to add to it.

She also knows that despite some people's behavior, most people mean well and want to work well with others. When incredibly difficult people must be dealt with, she avoids jumping on the negativity and instead figures out how to resolve the immediate concern. She feels that most problems can be solved by simply initiating a conversation. Since a great majority of people want to be viewed positively in the workplace, the odds are in her favor that addressing the issue will lead to a resolution. She doesn't worry about what happened last year, last week, or yesterday. She focuses on resolving the problem for the future with the goal of creating and sustaining peace at work.

In Conclusion

I hope that *Peace @ Work* has offered some helpful insights as well as an effective technique for handling conflicts on the job. The good news is that no matter how long you've been interacting in a passive, aggressive, or passive-aggressive manner, you can change that starting today if you wish.

The benefits will be a better sense of control, a sense of increased confidence about dealing with whatever problems may arise, decreased job stress, more positive relationships, and maybe even more success on the job and in the future.

How can you do this? Study GSSC, the four-part technique for handling interpersonal conflicts, and incorporate it into any conflict you have on the job. Remember to identify your goal, make it safe so the other person will listen and hear you, share your observations, perceptions, or feelings, and clarify and ask for an agreement moving forward.

In addition, no matter what gets thrown at you or how the other person reacts, remember the safety net and be prepared to ask questions to help understand what it will take to get to a resolution. The more you understand about the other person, the more capable you will be in coming to a resolution. You may also wind up with a more positive relationship.

Remember your overriding goal: to maintain positive relationships and solve problems moving forward. Why waste time focusing on what happened yesterday or the day before? Just problem-solve for the future and get back to working in peace.

It will be worth it.

THE GSSC TECHNIQUE IN OUTLINE FORM

STEP ONE:
IDENTIFY YOUR GOAL (G)

What do you want from the conversation?

STEP TWO:
MAKE IT SAFE FOR THE OTHER PERSON TO LISTEN TO YOU (S)

Begin by outlining your intent: you want to solve a problem, you need this person's help, and you appreciate this person and want to make sure you are working well together.

Use whatever feels safe and positive.

STEP THREE:
SHARE YOUR OBSERVATIONS, PERCEPTIONS, OR FEELINGS (S)

Avoid accusing, making charges, or making assumptions. You are not looking for a confession; you are trying to problem-solve and move forward.

Step Four:
Clarify and Ask for an Agreement Moving Forward (C)

Restate what you think you both heard and, if necessary, ask what you should do if the problem or issue occurs again.

Finally, as necessary, use the safety net of **asking questions** to help you better understand the other person and keep the conversation moving toward your goal. By remembering to simply ask questions that stay focused on your goal, you never have to worry about what the other person might say in response.

TROUBLESHOOTING COMMON QUESTIONS FROM EMPLOYEES

1. What if I ask to speak to a colleague and he/she refuses to talk with me?

Ask the person why he or she doesn't want to take the time to talk and see what the response is. Maybe this individual has a concern you were unaware of that you can address. Make sure your colleague knows you simply want to discuss something for the benefit of both of you. If this individual is totally determined to blow you off and refuses to speak with you, let the supervisor know about your concerns and what you've attempted. At least you will feel better for having tried. Teamwork and professional communication are everyone's responsibility. You want to rise above pettiness and problems and be seen as someone who is a good communicator and problem solver.

2. How do I know if an issue is worth bringing up? I don't
    need to bring up everything that irritates me.

If something happens that upsets you, make sure you take
the time to think about it before acting. Ask yourself what
really bothers you about the situation and whether you are
dealing with a rare occurrence or a potential pattern. If it's a
pattern, it's most likely worth discussing. Anything that can
negatively impact your working relationship is worth talking
about. There are times when we deal with people we probably
won't see much or have to interact with very often. We may
not feel it's important to talk to such individuals. As long as it
won't create further problems down the road, ignoring these
problems is reasonable.

3. What if I've talked to this person before and things
    improved for only a short time? Why should I bother
    trying again?

People are creatures of habit, and habits are very hard to break,
especially when you consider the fact that we're not always
aware of some of our bad habits. Good communicators realize
that behaviors seldom completely change after a single discussion. They know that change needs to be reinforced and that
when we want to help people make necessary changes, we
need to be persistent. We need to be willing to discuss the
issue again, as needed, so that it doesn't continue to create
problems.

4. Is there anything I can do to be proactive instead of just
    waiting for a problem to develop?

Yes. If there is someone you work closely with, ask him or her if there is one thing you can do to improve your working relationship or one thing you can do to make your work relationship even better. Honestly touching base and understanding the needs of others can be very helpful. The more you understand the people you work with, the more successful your relationships will be. After all, our work success depends heavily on our ability to develop and maintain positive work relationships.

5. This seems like a lot of work. Why should I even bother?

The relationships you have with your colleagues have a big impact on you. People who are straightforward and caring in their approach will have more positive relationships, will be well received by others, and will ultimately have less stress and more fun at work. Anyone who has worked in an office rife with backstabbing, gossiping, passive-aggressiveness, and underlying hostility knows the additional pain and stress it causes. Most people want to avoid this and can do so if they accept personal accountability. Addressing problems out in the open and working to resolve them is a key way to prevent such behavior and to increase the benefits that come with good teamwork. If you want to be successful and viewed as a strong team player or strong leader, it's critical that you work on your communication skills.

6. I've been pretty passive my whole life. How can I change a pattern of behavior I've had for so long?

You were not born passive. You may have developed this behavior over time, but it's not in your genes. This is learned behavior, and unless you are one of those people who does not feel a need to learn anything new, you are quite capable of becoming a more effective communicator. Anyone can learn these techniques any time they choose. After learning the key steps, practice your first conversation with someone at home first. You might be surprised at how much easier it is to initiate such a conversation when you are focused on a goal, when you start the conversation by making it safe, when you share your observations, perceptions, or feelings while avoiding accusations, when you clarify what is said and ask for an agreement going forward, and when you simply ask questions to better understand and focus on solving the problem moving forward.

ADDITIONAL EXAMPLES OF WORKPLACE CONFLICTS AND CONVERSATIONS

EXAMPLE 1

The conversations below between colleagues Alex and Sandra offer two very different takes on resolving a common conflict in the workplace. One approach is inflammatory and inadequate; the other is thoughtful and effective.

First is an example of what can happen when you do not have a positive goal in mind before beginning a conversation and when you fail to make it safe for the other person to hear you. Does this exchange sound familiar to conversations you've overheard or even participated in?

ALEX: Thanks for talking to me, Sandra. You know I'm responsible for coordinating the educational staff meetings each quarter, and it's a lot to handle. The reason I wanted to meet with you was to see what we could do about your being late to our staff meetings because it can be quite disruptive for our speakers.

SANDRA: What do you mean my being late?

ALEX: Come on, Sandra. You know you haven't made it on time to one staff meeting yet. You rush in about fifteen to twenty minutes late every time and disrupt things for everyone.

SANDRA: I disagree totally. Even if I'm late on rare occasions, there are several other people who regularly come in quite late. You should take a look at your own behavior. Most people I talk to can't stand attending the meetings in the first place, so maybe you need to consider what you can do to make the meetings more interesting.

ALEX: So this is what I get when I try to address a problem? You're pointing the finger at me? You're a piece of work, Sandra.

This conversation begins and ends poorly. What is Alex's goal? Does he want to point out Sandra's problem? Does he want Sandra to confess her sins?

Unfortunately, Alex neither begins with a clear goal in mind nor does he make it safe for Sandra to listen. If Alex's intent is to solve a problem and maintain a positive working relationship, he most certainly goes about it the wrong way.

On the other hand, if Alex had incorporated the four-part GSSC technique for handling interpersonal conflicts, the conversation would have gone something like this:

ALEX: Thanks for talking to me, Sandra. You know I'm responsible for coordinating the educational staff meetings each quarter, and it's a lot to handle. I need your help with something I've observed.

Alex's goal is to let Sandra know he's noticed she's been late to the meetings but also to explain why he needs her help with the issue. He starts off by making it safe for Sandra to listen and hear what he has to say by letting her know he needs her help.

SANDRA: Sure, what's up?

ALEX: As you know, we often have guest speakers at these meetings and it's important for us to start on time. It's my impression that you've been coming in late and I was wondering if there was something that can be done to help get you there at the start.

Alex shares his observations and perceptions with Sandra without making a direct accusation.

SANDRA: I haven't been coming in late, and if I have, it's only because I have other commitments. There are a lot of others you should be talking to, Alex.

ALEX: I understand how busy it can get, and I know you are not the only person who can run late. I just want to know if you would help me by trying to get there at the beginning? It's really important to me and sometimes it causes problems for the speakers and staff, and I don't want them to feel interrupted. Would you be willing to help me with this?

Alex avoids arguing about whether or not Sandra has been late and simply stays focused on his goal and on sharing his perspective.

His whole intention is to resolve the problem moving forward, and he does this by offering an explanation of why it's important.

SANDRA: I guess I'll try to be more aware. I didn't realize it was a problem. Again, I think you should talk to the others.

ALEX: I really appreciate your help with this, Sandra. Just so I'm clear, you plan to get to future staff meetings on time from now on. Is that correct?

Alex doesn't respond to Sandra's denial of the problem. Instead, he remains focused on his goal of seeing if Sandra is willing to help him resolve the problem by clarifying and asking for an agreement moving forward.

SANDRA: Yes, I'll make every effort to get there. I really didn't know it was that big of a deal, honestly. There may be times when it's something out of my control, but that shouldn't happen very often.

ALEX: Thanks a lot. I appreciate you helping me. If I do notice that there's a problem in the future, do you want me to let you know?

SANDRA: Sure. It may be due to some problem, and I wouldn't want you to think I'm doing this on purpose.

Alex makes sure he reiterates what he understands and that Sandra agrees with him. He also wants Sandra to give him permission to approach her again if there's a problem, which she does. This gives her an opportunity to explain what's going on, if necessary, and it gives him the opportunity to follow up if he needs to. If Alex does need to go to a higher level with the problem, he'll know he tried to solve it directly with Sandra first.

This conversation is a success because of the sensitive way in which Alex approaches the problem. The fact is, whenever you help someone understand a problem or why something is important, you are helping to solve the problem while simultaneously helping to preserve a working relationship. Many people will respond positively because they were unaware there was a problem in the first place and because you took the time and initiative to bring it to their attention in a respectful way.

EXAMPLE 2

Remember Bill and Sue's conversation in Chapter One about the guy at work who only talks about sports? Bill told Sue how everyone at work avoids him and Sue suggested that Bill talk to him, but Bill blew that suggestion off, saying it wouldn't help.

Since then, Bill has had a change of heart. He decides to talk to his colleague after all. He wants to find out what the obsession with sports is all about and whether or not this guy is even aware of how bad it is. Using the GSSC technique and remembering the secret weapon of communication, Bill finds himself working alone with the sports-obsessed guy one morning. No one else is around, so Bill initiates a conversation:

BILL: You know, Dwight, I have noticed something that I wanted to ask you about. You and I've been working together for a while now, and I was just curious about something.

DWIGHT: Sure, what?

BILL: I may be wrong, but it seems to me that you always talk about sports. I have never really noticed you talking about anything else.

DWIGHT: Oh. Do you have a problem with it?

BILL: I was just curious if you have other interests or if there is a reason that sports always come up?

DWIGHT: I just watch a lot of sports, that's all. What do you want me to talk about?

Dwight's tone is slightly defensive, so Bill offers an explanation that shares his perspective while furthering his goal of trying to figure his colleague out.

BILL: Well, you may not realize this, but I'm not big into sports.

DWIGHT: Seriously?

BILL: No, the only sport I pay attention to is golf, and now that I think about it, that's the one sport you never mention.

DWIGHT: (Laughs) Well, I'll be sure to bring up golf in the future. I don't always have to talk about sports, Bill. I just thought it was an easy way to start a conversation. I live alone, and I guess when I get to work I want to talk about what I watched on TV to try to fit it. Maybe I should start watching reality TV. I hear the boss and Sally are really into it.

BILL: No, if I were you, Dwight, I would just stick to sports.

By having this conversation, Bill realizes that the "sports-obsessed jerk" is actually a pretty nice guy who is trying his best to fit in. The two men soon become good friends and golf partners in the company league.

When Bill thinks back to his initial impression of Dwight, he has a hard time believing he was so shortsighted and unfair in his assessment. He's also very glad they had that brief conversation that seemed to change everything.

Example 3

Kathy has just finished her degree and has been hired to work in a department in the same company she worked in as an intern. This is Kathy's first professional job and she is quite excited. Unfortunately, another colleague in the department, Mary, has dampened some of her excitement. Mary has worked there for years, acts like she knows everything about everything, and loves to tell people what to do. Kathy quietly observed and put up with Mary's behavior for the first month, but now something has happened that she doesn't feel she can ignore.

Kathy has been told by several colleagues that Mary is badmouthing her behind her back, claiming that Kathy isn't doing her job, is lacking the experience she needs, and is an all-around bad hire.

Kathy thinks about the situation and asks herself what she wants. Initially, she decides to go to her boss to complain, but after thinking it over she decides to take another route. Talking to her supervisor first will only make it look like she can't address her own problems and it may create more problems with Mary down the road.

After sleeping on it, Kathy decides to have a conversation directly with Mary. She doesn't like or trust her right now, but she needs to work with her, and she decides it's better to rise above pettiness to try to solve this problem.

After giving it some more thought, Kathy decides her goal is to let Mary know she is aware of the negative things Mary is saying and to ask her to please come to her directly with any future concerns so that they can have a good working relationship.

At work that day, Kathy asks Mary if they can talk privately when Mary is free. Mary consents, and a short while later, they begin their discussion in a private office. Kathy speaks first:

KATHY: Mary, I appreciate you taking the time to talk to me. I've only worked here a short time, but it's really important to me that I have a good relationship with my colleagues. I'm hoping you can help me with something.

Kathy makes it safe for Mary to listen.

MARY: What?

KATHY: Well, I've heard that you may not be very happy with me working here.

Kathy shares her concerns by using "I've heard" rather than making a direct accusation.

MARY: Where do you get that?

KATHY: Well, you know how people talk and how things get around. I've heard that you were not very happy that I was hired and that you have concerns about my work.

MARY: Who told you that?

KATHY: I've heard it from various people, and I just want to ask you if there is a problem.

MARY: No, not at all. People shouldn't spread rumors like that. I've never said anything negative about anyone around here.

KATHY: Well, I'm glad to hear that. I hope that if you have a concern about me, my work, or something you think I've done incorrectly, that you will let me know. I'm totally open to talking with you about any problems. Just let me know if you would, please.

Kathy doesn't get into whether or not things were said. Her goal is not to hear a confession from Mary. Her goal is to simply let her know that she is hearing things and that she would like for Mary to come to her with any concerns in the future.

MARY: Of course I would. I have no problem with you at all, Kathy. It's actually Sally who causes me problems. She's really something else.

KATHY: Well, I just want to make sure that you will come to me if you have a problem and that you don't feel any need to talk to others about me. Do you agree that you'll let me know if something comes up that you have a concern about?

Kathy stays focused on her goal and doesn't address the Sally issue at all. She reinforces what she is looking for and asks a question to clarify.

MARY: Of course.

KATHY: I appreciate it, and if I hear anything else in the future, I'll be sure to let you know, Mary.

Kathy reinforces the agreement by nicely letting Mary know she'll be back if the behavior continues.

MARY: Please do.

In the short run, it would have been very easy for Kathy to focus on her anger or run to her supervisor or even other colleagues to obtain support. Instead, Kathy wisely decides it's in her best interests to deal with the situation in an assertive manner. She talks to Mary in a very straightforward yet kind and respectful manner while focusing on solving the problem moving forward.

Mary now knows she isn't dealing with a pushover, and she will probably think twice before saying anything negative about Kathy again. If she does slip up, Kathy will surely talk to her again and may even take the problem further if necessary.

What actually happens is that, over time, Kathy and Mary develop a pretty nice and respectful working relationship. Mary may be a pain for others to deal with, but from Kathy's perspective, her relationship with her co-worker is pleasant, professional, and based on mutual respect.

Example 4

People in positions of power and authority can most certainly make demanding conversations more difficult. The health care environment can be particularly prone to this challenge because of the critical work that occurs, the teamwork that is required, the pressures and stress levels individuals feel, the time intensiveness they must commit to, the various personalities involved, and of course the hierarchy.

One of my favorite examples of someone in health care who was faced with a very difficult situation was shared with me many years ago. Following a presentation, I was approached by a medical resident who wanted to tell me how she had been assertive with a physician she was having trouble with. She told me she had been in the examining room with a patient doing an initial assessment when the senior physician entered the room and proceeded to berate her. This wasn't the first time this had happened. In fact, the resident had been having trouble with this physician for several weeks.

I was intrigued to hear how she had handled this, and she told me she had politely asked the physician if they could talk in the room next door, to which the senior physician agreed.

At this point, I was quite impressed with the example of calm assertiveness shown by the young physician. This most certainly would end well, I thought.

Then this young doctor pointed her finger in my face and said, "And then I told him, 'Don't you ever talk to me that way in front of a patient again! If you have a problem with something I've done, you can talk to me privately.'"

When my shock abated, I asked if she really thought this was an assertive response, to which she responded affirmatively. I then asked if it had worked, to which she replied, "Why yes, he never did it again."

I remember standing there feeling perplexed. This certainly was not an approach I would recommend, and I was stunned to hear it had led to a positive outcome. As I was mulling this over, she added, "Except, he has influence on my performance appraisal, and I really think he's taking it out on me now."

Ah. Immediately, the situation made sense. Because bullies don't usually respond well to other people trying to bully them back, I now frequently highlight the common confusion regarding aggressive versus assertive behavior in my presentations. Assertive people do not point fingers, use loud or negative tones in their voices, or attempt to put people "in their place." On the contrary, they speak with respect and consideration for other people's feelings, and the outcome tends to be much more positive.

Here's an example of how this young resident could have better handled the same situation utilizing the GSSC technique, beginning with the senior physician entering the room.

SENIOR PHYSICIAN: I thought I asked you to let me know when Ms. Camp was here! You need to keep me better informed from now on.

RESIDENT: My apologies for the misunderstanding.

For the time being, the resident puts aside her feelings and focuses on the patient. Later, using good timing and privacy, she asks the senior physician if she can talk privately with him. She had hoped to avoid this, but he has been creating a great deal of additional stress for her. Her goal is to find out if he is willing to make an adjustment in how he communicates with her when there is a problem. He agrees to see her in his office, and this is how their conversation goes.

RESIDENT: I appreciate your time very much. I am learning a great deal here, and I want you to know how much I appreciate the effort you are putting into helping with my residency. I have a concern about something I am hoping you can help me with.

(She makes it safe for the senior physician to listen.)

SENIOR PHYSICIAN: What's up?

RESIDENT: I'm not sure if you are aware of this, but I've noticed there are times when you seem to get very angry with me. Yesterday was a good example. You appeared quite angry when you entered the room with the patient, and I felt bad that I had no idea what I'd done wrong.

(The resident shares her perception while avoiding an accusation.)

Senior physician: Maybe you need thicker skin.

Resident: I'm just trying to find out if there is anything that can be done to improve our communication. I understand there are times when you might be angry or upset, but I am hoping there is something we can do to prevent having such times in front of other people. I would be happy to address any concerns you have in private.

(She ignores the negative comment and stays focused on the goal.)

Senior physician: Are you accusing me of upsetting our patients now?

Resident: No, not at all. I just want you to know that I'm happy to talk to you privately any time there are things I could be doing better or differently. I'm just asking if we could prevent others, either patients or staff members, from witnessing any problems with our communication.

(The resident doesn't get off track by the anger of the physician and stays focused on the goal.)

Senior physician: Well, I don't know what you are talking about. It's my job to teach you, and that sometimes involves giving you constructive feedback.

Resident: I totally understand and agree. It would just be very helpful for me if I could get the feedback and coaching privately. For example, if something like yesterday's incident happens again, would you be willing to either talk to me after we are done with the patient or ask me to step in another room?

(The resident asks a question, staying focused on the goal.)

SENIOR PHYSICIAN: You need to pull me in quicker with the patients. I really hate getting behind, so speed things up on your end. Maybe that will help.

RESIDENT: So part of what is bothering you is the pace? I will certainly make an effort to be more timely in the future. Thank you. And just so I'm clear, if you need to give me constructive feedback in the future, you'll pull me aside or wait for a private moment to let me know, correct?

(The resident seeks clarification and an agreement moving forward.)

SENIOR PHYSICIAN: I'll do what I can. I don't think there will be a problem if you pick up the pace.

RESIDENT: Thank you. I appreciate this very much.

In talking to the senior physician, the resident learns that he really hates getting behind. The fact that she is one of the fastest residents does not matter to the young doctor. It's not important if what the physician said is true or not. By focusing on the goal of the conversation, the resident understands that the physician's anger could stem from a variety of things. Because she has made him aware of the problem and has politely asked him to help resolve it moving forward, the odds are pretty good that he will do so.

On the other hand, had the resident avoided this discussion, the problem would have continued and perhaps worsened, and she probably would not have understood why or what she could do to positively influence the situation. Even though the resident feels she works quickly, she will be sensitive to the senior physician's concern and will even ask in the future if she is meeting his expectations. Also, if the problem happens again, she knows she can talk to him about it. If she focuses on what she can do to help resolve the problem and avoids accusations or putting the senior physician on the defensive, she can come to a positive resolution for both of them.

A BRIEF QUESTIONNAIRE FOR REVIEW

1. What is the most important step to remember in the GSSC communication technique?

    A. Asking questions

    B. The goal

    C. Making it safe to hear

    D. Clarifying an agreement

2. Deb would like to talk to her supervisor and request his help in prioritizing assignments. She tried to have this discussion before but somehow she wound up with more work and no help in setting her priorities. What is a reasonable goal for this conversation?

    A. To obtain assistance for some of her projects

B. To get her supervisor to understand the stress she is under

C. To obtain her supervisor's help in prioritizing assignments

D. To improve their working relationship

3. Bob uses the GSSC technique to talk to his colleague, Rick, about his habit of taking overly long lunch breaks, which leaves his co-workers shouldering his responsibilities until he returns. Bob is focused on his goal of finding out if Rick is willing to resolve this problem. He starts off by making it safe, but despite that, Rick makes the following statement: "Who are you to talk to me about my break? Are you my boss or something?" What is the best response for Bob based on the GSSC technique?

A. No, I'm not your boss. I'm sorry you don't want to have a conversation about this.

B. No, I'm not your boss, but I'm trying to figure out how to get past this problem. Are you saying you won't work it out with me?

C. No, I'm not your boss. Forget it. It's not worth getting upset over.

D. No, I'm not your boss, but I guess I'll need to talk to the boss to solve this problem.

4. Will suspects his supervisor is not happy with him. Ever since he talked to human resources about a problem with his paycheck, he's noticed that Susan is avoiding him. She talks to his co-workers freely, but not to him, and the other day she actually passed him in the hallway without

acknowledging him. Will doesn't want this to continue and he decides that his goal is to find out if there is a problem and, if so, what he can do to resolve it. What would be a good statement to make the conversation safe for Susan to listen to him?

A. It's important to me that we have a good working relationship, and I am feeling very uncomfortable in your presence lately.

B. I've noticed that you've not been talking to me lately as usual and the other day you walked by me without even making eye contact. Can you tell me if there is a problem?

C. You've appeared to be upset by ignoring me recently and I just want to find out if there is a problem.

D. As my supervisor, it's really important to me that you and I have a good relationship. I've noticed some changes lately, and I'm wondering if there is any concern on your part.

5.   Which is the best example of Will sharing his perspective with Susan?

A. I've noticed that you are ignoring me and treating me differently than the rest of the team.

B. You don't seem like yourself lately, and I feel very uncomfortable as a result.

C. The last few times I saw you, I got the impression you may be upset with me. I just had a feeling that you were hesitant to talk to me.

    D. You are treating me differently than the rest of
the team, and I am hoping that I didn't do something to upset you.

The Answers

1. The most important step in the communication process
   is to identify the goal before beginning the conversation
   (B). If you do not do this, it can easily make everything
   that follows more difficult. Conversations get off track,
   you can be manipulated, and you will have a hard time
   asking important questions if the other person goes on the
   attack. Identifying the goal is the true core of the GSSC
   communication technique.

2. Deb's primary goal is to get her supervisor's help in
   prioritizing her work (C). The other options may have
   some connection to the discussion, but they aren't the
   true focus. Deb needs help in prioritizing, and if her boss
   refuses such help, Deb can be prepared to ask questions
   to get back to her original goal.

3. The best response when confronted aggressively is to ask a
   question, so (B) is the answer. You may still be shut down,
   but at least you can feel good about trying to resolve the
   problem, especially if and when you approach your supervisor for help.

4. The best way to help people feel safe and open to hearing
   what you have to say is to help them understand your
   intent to resolve a problem. The best choice for this is

(D) because Will states that his intention is to have a good relationship and he avoids giving Susan a reason to get defensive. The first answer starts off okay but then Will accuses Susan of making him uncomfortable. The other choices also appear quite accusatory. Remember, if you want people to listen to you, you need to help them be comfortable. Accusations do not have that relaxing impact on others.

5. The best way to share is to focus on your impression, your observations, your thoughts, or your feelings. This is best done in response (C), and the key is the use of the word "impression." The final answer may end okay, but it begins with an accusation, as do all the others. Accusing people typically leads to defensiveness and possibly more conflict. Remember, you are not looking for a confession; you are simply trying to resolve a problem moving forward.

ACKNOWLEDGMENTS

I have a number of people to thank for assistance with this book, beginning with my parents. I would like to give special thanks to my father, Robert Camp, who helped me with his repeated readings, suggestions, and support. I also want to acknowledge my late mother Gisela, who gave up early on the idea of a career for herself in order to make sure her three kids could achieve one.

I also want to thank my partner and CEO extraordinaire Nancy Schlichting, who is always there for me, as well as my children Allie and Nick Theisen.

I also want to recognize the support of my brothers Terry and Steve Camp and sisters-in-law Katie and Heidi, who gave great advice and encouragement throughout the project. I want to also mention my nieces and nephew, Lindsay, Naomi, Mackenzie, Maddie, Joe, and Rosie who also inspired me. Especially my niece Naomi, who at one point told me the book was "awesome."

I can never thank my family sufficiently, because even if they did not help directly, they are always a source of incredible inspiration for me. The same is true of my friends. Among those who took the time to read *Peace at Work* and offer advice are Julie Copits, Barb Czopek , Ronnie Hall, Kris Harvey, Hillary Herring, Sandy Herring, Patrick Irwin, Kathy Macki, Debbie Saoud, Karen Snow, Karen Young, and Karla Zarb.

I also want to give special thanks to Mr. Gail Warden, who was kind enough to offer some great pointers for the book as well as his testimonial. Besides Gail, I also want to give special thanks to the other wonderful and very busy people who took the time to write a testimonial: Dr. Bill Conway, Gerard Van Grinsven, Katie Kessler, Kathy Oswald, Sandy Pierce, and Jane Struder.

Another key person who helped tremendously in this book becoming a reality is Rebecca Chown, my editor. I had the good fortune of briefly meeting Becky one day and a year later asked if she could help me with this project. I'm not quite sure the book would ever have happened without her help and very positive influence.

Another group to thank are the amazing people who work in health care and especially those at Henry Ford Health System. It takes special people to care for those in need with grace, skill, and compassion. I'm continuously grateful for the opportunity to work with such incredibly inspiring people.

ABOUT THE AUTHOR

Pam Theisen has a passion for helping people be successful in their jobs. She has spent many years assisting employees and managers with a variety of problems in the workplace. Pam is an experienced counselor and coach who believes that communication problems and conflicts on the job create a high amount of unnecessary stress in the workplace.

She has worked in health care for more than thirty years in various clinical and leadership positions including medical social work in oncology and transplant, employee assistance program management, human resources, organizational development, and clinic administration.

In July 2010, Pam founded her own business, PT Consulting Group, a training program and individual coaching group, specializing in communication and conflict resolution.

Pam has a bachelor's degree in psychology from Western Michigan University and a master's degree in social work from the University of Michigan. She is a licensed MSW and is certified as a Senior Human Resource Professional.

Pam can be reached through the website: www. PT-Consulting-Group.com.